# VANISHING KINGDOMS
The Irish Chiefs and their Families

*For John and James*

# Vanishing Kingdoms

## *The Irish Chiefs and their Families*

WALTER J.P. CURLEY

*Foreword by* CHARLES LYSAGHT

*Portraits by* GORDON WETMORE

THE LILLIPUT PRESS
DUBLIN

First published 2004 by
THE LILLIPUT PRESS
62–63 Sitric Road, Arbour Hill,
Dublin 7, Ireland
www.lilliputpress.ie



A CIP record for this title is available from
The British Library.

1 3 5 7 9 10 8 6 4 2

ISBN 1 84351 055 3 (pbk)
1 84351 056 1 (hbk)

Set in 11 on 13 pt Bembo
Printed by Colour Books Ltd., Dublin

# Contents

**Claimants to the high kingship*

# Illustrations

PORTRAITS
*by* Gordon Wetmore

# Acknowledgments

I am grateful to the descendants of the Irish kings, chiefs of the name, and to their families, who received me and the artist Gordon Wetmore with a high level of co-operation – and hospitality. Also, from the outset of the project, Verette and William Finlay, former chairman of the National Gallery and governor of the Bank of Ireland, gave me guidance and counsel; and later, Desmond FitzGerald, Knight of Glin, provided an additional critical eye and bracing candour to the developing manuscript.

John Campbell and Richard Ryan, former Irish ambassadors to France, Spain, Portugal, and the United Nations, made substantive contributions to my research. And I am delighted that author, historian and friend Charles Lysaght provided such keen insight and reflections in his Foreword.

My cherished long-time associate, Eleanor Bennett of New York, who can spot a split infinitive from twenty paces, transcribed the text with rare prowess and patience. I was also fortunate to have the support of Billy Murphy of Limerick – photo-historian, philosopher, and expert driver – who transported us around Ireland during our visits to the hereditary chiefs.

The initial catalyst for this book was my old colleague, J. Mabon Childs of Pennsylvania, whose portrait had been painted by Gordon Wetmore.

I am indebted to the many helpful people in Ireland who were intrigued by (and often related to) the ancient dynastic families. Fortunately, my own immediate family in America – daughter Peggy Curley Wiles, a teacher; daughter-in-law Jane Bayard Curley, an art historian; and son Patrick, an architect – also lent their professional skills and judgment to the project.

As this book developed, Antony Farrell, editor-in-chief of The Lilliput Press, gave me the crucial benefit of his erudition along with his friendship.

In the final analysis, *Vanishing Kingdoms: The Irish Chiefs and their Families* would not exist without the historian's eye, good humour, and enduring encouragement provided by my dear wife, Mary Walton Curley.

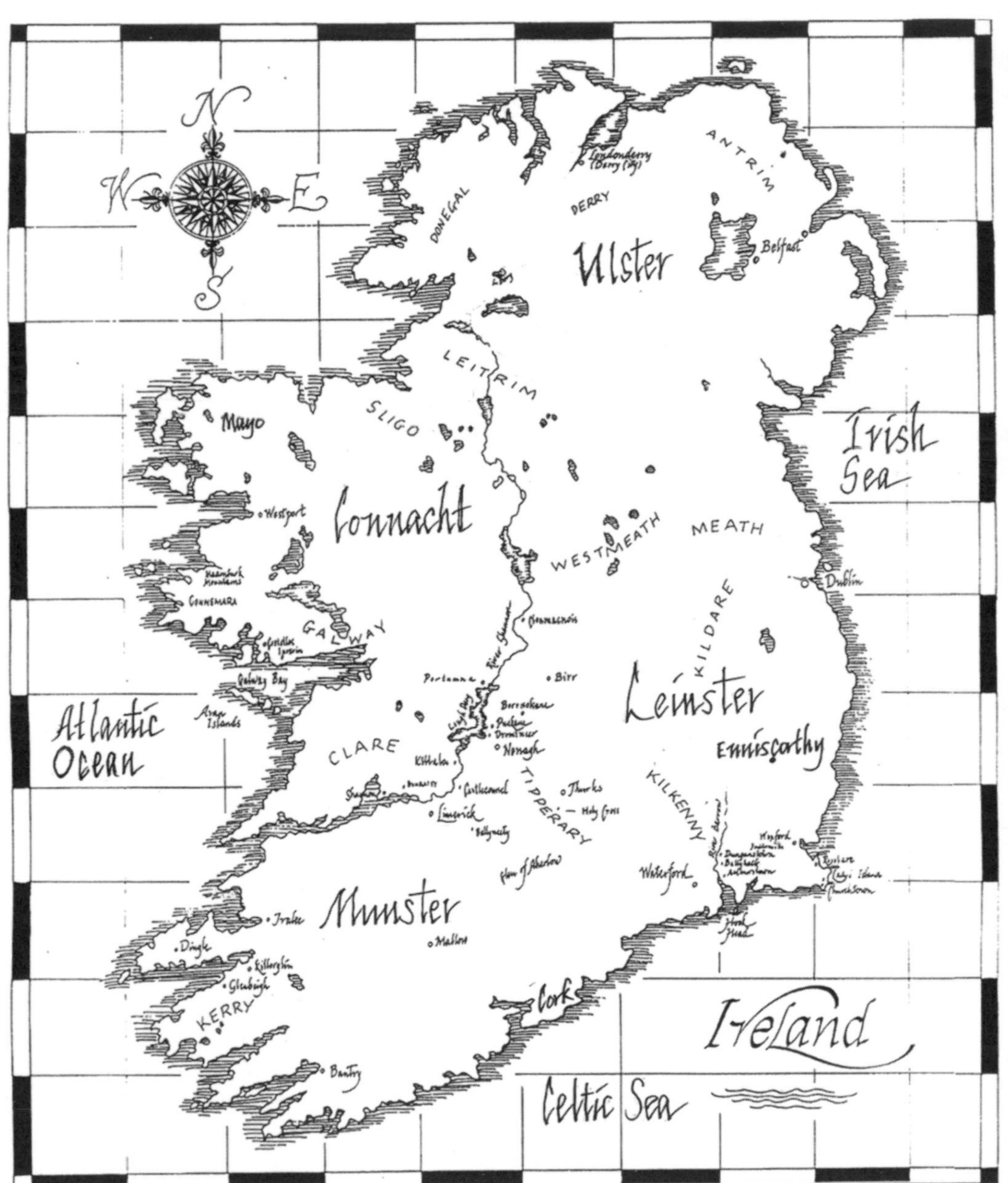

N
W
E
S
ANTRIM
Londonderry (Derry City)
DERRY
DONEGAL
Ulster
Belfast
LEITRIM
SLIGO
Mayo
Irish Sea
Connacht
Westport
WESTMEATH
MEATH
Dublin
CONNEMARA
GALWAY
KILDARE
River Shannon
Portumna
Birr
Galway Bay
Aran Islands
Leinster
Atlantic Ocean
CLARE
Nenagh
Enniscorthy
TIPPERARY
Thurles
Holy Cross
KILKENNY
Limerick
Waterford
Wexford
Munster
Tralee
Mallow
Dingle
Hook Head
Cork
KERRY
Bantry
Ireland
Celtic Sea

# Foreword

As a people we Irish are often oblivious to what is most interesting and valuable about ourselves until some well-disposed visitor draws it to our attention. There can be few visitors as well disposed to Ireland as Walter Curley, whom I first met at Clonalis, the seat of the O'Conor Don in 1976 on the very day that his friend the British Ambassador Christopher Ewart-Biggs was assassinated in Dublin. Walter Curley was then United States Ambassador to Ireland and had long been the proud owner of a house in Mayo. He later became Ambassador in Paris. He retained his Irish connection as a director of the Bank of Ireland and as a frequent visitor, always glad to assist Irish people or their projects. It is interesting that the Ambassador should be drawn to the living descendants of the Gaelic chieftains as a noteworthy feature of our national life. It is also opportune at a time when our government, through the Genealogical Office, has decided to terminate the official recognition of them, initiated in 1944, that reached its apotheosis when President Mary Robinson received the Standing Council of Chiefs and Chieftains after their inaugural meeting in 1991.

Apart from the general human interest in ancestry and in the vicissitudes of families, the chieftains link modern Ireland with the ancient Gaelic order that preceded the English conquest and remind us that we are an ancient nation that had our own culture and, what was then synonymous, our own aristocracy. The long struggle to reassert an Irish national identity can only be understood against this background; it was the struggle of those who were dispossessed not just oppressed.

So it was that the founding fathers of the independent state placed emphasis on preserving what was left of the old Gaelic Ireland, whether it took the form of ancient monuments or the Irish language. They even flirted with the revival of the Brehon Law but this proved impracticable. The courtesy recognition given to the descendants of the Gaelic chieftains after

1944 by the Genealogical Office that took over the Office of Arms was of a piece with this. It is interesting that Mr de Valera, who had come to the national movement through the Gaelic League, gave his personal approval to the project when it was put to him by the first Chief Herald, a fellow Gaelgeoir Edward MacLysaght. A decade later, as Chancellor of the National University, de Valera was pleased to confer an honorary degree on the lineal descendant of the ancient O'Donnells who was the Duke of Tetuan in the nobility of Spain.

The chieftains surveyed by Ambassador Curley in this engaging volume may be seen as a microcosm of the fate of the upper class of the old Gaelic order. There were those who accepted the opening to integrate themselves into the new English Protestant Ascendancy established as part of the conquest of Ireland in the sixteenth and seventeenth centuries. There were those who departed Ireland rather than accept this new order and became part of the aristocracies of the Catholic powers of continental Europe. There were those who hung on as minor Catholic gentry and they are rightly celebrated. They produced from their number several leading nineteenth-century figures, notably our first great political leader, the Liberator Daniel O'Connell, who thus personified the link between the old Gaelic order and the modern Irish democracy. But it is clear that a vast number of chieftain families either died out or, more probably, descended into such obscurity and illiteracy that their lineage cannot easily be traced from documentary sources.

That there must have been a large class of dispossessed Irish Catholic gentry is evidenced by an early eighteenth-century Act that criminalized 'all loose idle vagrants and such as pretend to be Irish gentlemen and will not work'. The best authenticated example of social descent of this kind is the case of The McSweeney Doe, whose early nineteenth-century ancestor, a travelling tinsmith, was identified to the antiquarian John O'Donovan and whose dynastic claim was under consideration by the Chief Herald in 2003 when the decision was taken to terminate courtesy recognition. The uncertainty engendered by the likely social descent of many of those of chieftain stock was, of course, a ripe breeding ground for bogus claims of all sorts. Equally, it was probably the case that the presence among the downtrodden Irish peasantry of the descendants of the old chieftain caste must have contributed to the sense of dispossession that was to fuel the Irish nationalist movement and to distinguish it from normal social egalitarian movements.

Edward MacLysaght inherited a situation where a list of chieftains had long been published annually in *Thom's Directory* and *Whitaker's Almanac*, which stated that they were not officially recognized but had become recognized by courtesy. They were The Fox, The MacCarthy Reagh, The MacDermot, The MacDermot-Roe, The McGillycuddy of the Reeks, The

O'Callaghan, O'Conor Don, The O'Donoghue of the Glens, The O'Doneven of Clerahan, The O'Donovan, The O'Grady, The O'Mahony of Kerry, The O'Kelly of Hy-Maine, The O'Morchoe, The O'Neill, The O'Rourke, The O'Shee, and The O'Toole. It is noteworthy that others who used the designation 'The' at that time, such as O'Phelan, Chief of the Decies, The MacEgan, The O'Brenan or The O'Rahilly, were not included.

MacLysaght considered that it was important to authenticate genealogically the claims of all those using the designation 'The' in order to expose those who were bogus. With the assistance of a keen genealogist called Terence Gray all claimants were examined to ascertain if they could prove descent on the eldest male line from the last chiefs of the name. Of those listed in *Thom's,* a number did not pass muster; they were The MacCarthy Reagh, The O'Callaghan (Colonel O'Callaghan-Westropp), The O'Doneven of Clerahan, The O'Mahony of Kerry, The O'Rourke and The O'Shee. The MacDermot Roe was found to have been dormant since 1917. A notice was placed in the official government gazette, *Iris Oifigiúil*, in December 1944 listing ten chiefs of the name. In the case of two others, The O'Grady of Kilballyowen and The O'Kelly of Gallagh and Tycooly, it was stated that, while not chieftainries in the strict sense, they had a legal right to their title having been long styled under these designations, and that their pedigrees, duly authenticated, were on record in the Genealogical Office. In the following year The O'Morchoe was listed together with two others who had not been included in *Thom's*, namely, The O'Brien of Thomond, who was Lord Inchiquin and The O'Donel of Tir Connell, a Dublin civil servant who had not sought recognition before being informed of his entitlement by the Chief Herald. Other chiefs of the name were recognized under succeeding chief heralds while The O'Toole became dormant on the death of the French count of the name, leaving us with the twenty included in this book.

It was an objection to MacLysaght's action that succession to Gaelic chieftainries under Brehon Law was governed not by primogeniture but by a system of tanistry, under which an heir apparent (called *tánaise*) was chosen by the immediate family group of the existing chieftain extending to second cousins, known as the *derbhfine.**

MacLysaght's justification was that the system of primogeniture had become the general rule before the end of the Gaelic Order and that what

* *The point has been made that the action was contrary to the legislation that had abolished Gaelic chieftains, which had been carried over into the law of the independent Irish State in 1922 with the rest of the law then in force. However, it could be countered that the legislation abolishing the Gaelic chieftainaries was of a racial character that would have precluded its being carried over into the domestic law of the independent Irish State that traced its legitimacy on the Proclamation of an Irish Republic in Easter 1916, which claimed a continuity between the Irish Republic and the old Gaelic nation.*

he was doing had the merit of distinguishing those with reasonable ancestral claims from those who were bogus. The courtesy recognition given was, he pointed out, clearly stated to be no more than a statement of genealogical fact. At a practical level it would not have been possible to revive the Brehon law of succession retrospectively. To begin again to apply it with future effect, as was suggested in 1998 by the Standing Council of Chiefs and Chieftains, would have little logic.

Ironically, the objective of avoiding bogus claims that had been MacLysaght's motivation, was frustrated when in 1989 MacLysaght's second next successor as Chief Herald, Donal Begley, recognized Terence MacCarthy as The MacCarthy Mór on the basis of a pedigree registered as authentic by his predecessor Gerard Slevin. The recognition was withdrawn in 1999 when it was established that the pedigree had been registered in reliance on a forged letter. This, as Ambassador Curley indicates at various points, has cast a shadow over at least some of those who were recognized about the same time, and enquiries were initiated by the Chief Herald.

Finally in 2003 the Chief Herald Brendan O'Donoghue decided that the practice of granting courtesy recognition as chief of the name should be discontinued, and that no further action should be taken in relation to the applications on hand for courtesy recognition, or in relation to the review of certain cases in which recognition was granted in the years 1989-95.

This decision was stated to be based on advice received from the Office of the Attorney General that:

> There is not, and never was, any statutory or legal basis for the practice of granting courtesy recognition as chief of the name;
>
> In the absence of an appropriate basis in law, the practice of granting courtesy recognition should not be continued by the Genealogical Office; and
>
> Even if a sound legal basis for the system existed, it would not be permissible for me to review and reverse decisions made by a previous Chief Herald except in particular situations, for example, where decisions were based on statements or documents which were clearly false or misleading in material respects.

The decision of the Chief Herald to withdraw from the business of designating chieftains for courtesy recognition is understandable in the light of what had occurred. But it must be questioned if it is responsible for the Chief Herald to relinquish his responsibilities leaving questions over the official authentication given to those recognized in recent decades. It is a pity that the full legal option of the Office of the Attorney General was not published as the account given implies that because there was no specific statutory basis for granting courtesy recognition as chief of the name it had no basis in law. This is a *non sequitur.* In law, a function of a government department does not have to have a specific statutory basis to be legal. There are many activities of government departments that have no statutory basis other than the annual Appropriation Act and the fact that they are within the general functions of the departments concerned. The authentication of pedigrees was among the functions of the Office of Arms taken over by the Genealogical Office in 1943 and, as such, must be regarded as being a legitimate activity unless precluded by statute. Insofar as the courtesy recognition of a chief of the name was no more than an authentication of a pedigree, it had a clear legal basis.

At this juncture it is, I think, essential to disentangle the issue of courtesy recognition from that of the authentication of pedigrees and to decide what should be done about each. It is difficult to give a precise meaning to the concept of courtesy recognition but it probably means nothing more than that in courtesy one addresses a person by the name by which they are generally known. The law sets no limits to the names by which a person may be known. While the Constitution states that titles of nobility shall not be conferred by the State and that no titles of nobility or honour may be accepted by any citizen except with the prior approval of the government, it has never been the law that citizens or other people may not use titles in this State; indeed, this has been done even in official contexts. All this may create difficulties for governments because use of a name may be prayed in aid as a form of recognition, especially if used on passports or other official documents. The whole issue, like the thorny issue of precedence, needs to be addressed authoritatively. But, meanwhile, if recognition is accorded to titles conferred by English or British kings and queens of Ireland and to those conferred by foreign sovereigns, including the Pope, it may be questioned if it is right to withhold the courtesy of recognition to names used by those certified by the Chief Herald to be descended from a Gaelic chieftain.

The authentication of pedigrees was achieved under the system of registered pedigrees verified and authenticated by the Ulster King-of-Arms and, after 1943, by the Chief Herald. This facility was withdrawn in recent years and the Genealogical Office now examines pedigrees only in the context of confirming if a person is entitled to arms previously granted. That the Chief Herald should no longer register pedigrees as authentic in the Genealogical Office seems to belie the central function incorporated in the title of the office. It is surely in the public interest that there should be some official body that authenticates pedigrees. As part of a general function of authenticating pedigrees it would be proper to validate the line of those claiming to be descended from Gaelic chieftains. This is, incidentally, no more than the

Ulster King-of-Arms was prepared to do in the eighteenth century for the descendants of the Gaelic nobility – the Wild Geese – who emigrated to continental Europe. If their pedigrees are authenticated, those choosing to name themselves in the style of a Gaelic chieftain would then be able to refer to this in their entries in books of reference. This was the position before 1943. It may be suggested that the Chief Herald should authenticate descent in the female line from Gaelic chieftains – one thinks of the descent of the Esmondes from the O'Flaherty chieftains of Iar-Chonnacht and of the More O'Ferralls from the O'More chieftains of Leix. In this age of transparency it would also be appropriate that authenticated pedigrees should be a matter of public record so that scholars and other interested parties have access to the material upon which they are based.

In the absence of any authentication of Gaelic pedigrees by the Chief Herald in the Genealogical Office, the Council of Chiefs and Chieftains may arrogate the function to themselves. This would not be altogether satisfactory in view of the queries that have been raised about the pedigrees of some of its members. Otherwise, those seeking to authenticate such pedigrees and, indeed, other Irish pedigrees, may have to resort to the Ulster King-of-Arms in London. This would be humiliating for the Genealogical Office and defeat the very purpose for which it was established.

To have compounded the withdrawal of courtesy recognition with a discontinuance of the authentication of pedigrees going back before the English conquest breaks a link between the modern Irish State and the old Gaelic nation, and is a strange action in a country that, as Ambassador Curley rightly points out, boasts some of the oldest authenticated pedigrees in Europe. The action taken may be seen as symbolic of the fact that the modern inclusive Ireland no longer seeks justification for its existence in an identification with the old Gaelic nation. It may be healthy that we do not attempt to identify modern Ireland only with the Gaelic tradition. But neither should we go to the opposite extreme of neglecting or rejecting that tradition. In the long run no nation is enriched in the eyes of the world if it turns its back on its roots. This delightful book directs our attention to the antiquity of our roots for which we should be grateful.

CHARLES LYSAGHT
*Dublin, September 2004*

# Introduction

Royalty and hereditary nobility hold a certain fascination for many ordinary citizens (or subjects, as the case may be). Emotions on the matter range from admiration, deep dedication, and often sycophancy, to curiosity, envy and aversion. At all social and intellectual levels, in virtually every culture, a part of our human intellect seems to be beguiled by the hereditarily select. Ireland is no exception.

Much of the seductive aura clinging to these figures and families stems from the power that usually accompanies sovereignty and historic entitlement. In varying degrees many people are intrigued by the intricate skeins of bloodlines and politics; even when the power has been long removed, the mystique often continues in an enduring after-glow.

In 2004 Europe has ten hereditary sovereign states – kingdoms and principalities: Belgium, Denmark, Liechtenstein, Luxembourg, the Netherlands, Monaco, Norway, Spain, Sweden and the United Kingdom. Only ninety years ago at the outbreak of World War I there were thirty-five reigning European monarchs, and only four European republics – France, Portugal, Switzerland and San Marino. Today, only twenty-nine hereditary sovereignties in the world are still 'in business': in addition to the ten Europeans, the total includes, in Africa, Lesotho, Morocco and Swaziland; in the Middle East, Bahrain, Jordan, Kuwait, Oman, Qatar, Saudi Arabia and the United Arab Emirates; and in Asia, Bhutan, Brunei, Cambodia, Japan, Malaysia, Nepal, Thailand, Tonga and Western Samoa.

A century ago British social scientist Walter Bagehot wrote: 'Above all, royalty is to be reverenced. In its mystery is its life; we must not let day light in upon the magic.' Many times in history, however, the 'day light' has arrived with sudden devastation and sweeping changes. Although monarchies that have been toppled are ostensibly relegated to the dustbins of history – in the case of Ireland, centuries ago – the memories, the auras, and the magnetism seem to linger on. They survive most persistently in continental Europe where some former monarchs (as well as valid Claimants to the empty thrones) await patiently a call to return; these figures are not only *de jure* the keepers of the royal flame, but are often the focal points of active political movements bent on returning the lapsed nations to the monarchical system. A shiver of hope charged through diverse royal veins-in-exile in 1983 when the son of Don Juan, Count of Barcelona – the Bourbon Pretender – was returned as His Majesty King Juan Carlos I to the throne of Spain, which had been empty since his grandfather, King Alfonso XIII, was ousted in 1931. Another glimmer of optimism encouraged the royal exiles when former King Simeon of Bulgaria, who lost his throne in 1946, became Prime Minister of his homeland in 2001.

Royalty-watchers everywhere keenly follow the pomp, circumstance and minutiae of the currently ruling families and of the nobles surrounding them in the system. These happenings are regularly in the media – and some have relevance. It is impossible to calculate accurately the positive financial impact, for example, that the British monarchy has on tourism, or the negative effects that its dissolution would have on the entire economy of the United Kingdom; all political parties in Great Britain readily concede that the mere existence of the monarchy has enormous economic influence on their country's well-being. While this benefit is not, *per se*, an overwhelming justification for that particular form of government, it is certainly not a trivial factor in it.

The choice between a dynastic monarchical system and a republican or other governing process has been discussed for centuries. Historians, politicians and ordinary people in many parts of the world, by their very natures, will assure that this debate persists on into the future. (Even in the American presidential primary campaigns in the Spring of 2000, semantic echoes of the old argument about dynasties were heard in the rhetoric of the opponents of George W. Bush, the governor of Texas, during his battle to become the Republican Party's nominee for the White House: opponents repeatedly called for 'an election not a coronation'.) Whether the monarchs are incumbent or merely hopeful, the enchantment of the royals and their descendants for many people remains undiminished.

Americans are most familiar with the names and styles of European royalty and nobility – especially those in Britain; for generations English lords and ladies, along with the royal dukes and princes, have been striding, sashaying, fox-trotting and galloping through countless novels, plays, films and, indeed, through the personal lives of many Americans. That aristocratic segment of British society is still well entrenched: titles abound and new ones continue to be granted by Queen Elizabeth II, a sovereign whose own special status endures with unfailing fascination for knights and commoners alike. The Anglo-Saxon monarchy, although buffeted in recent years both by scandal and pedestrian behaviour within the royal family itself and by outbursts of native English republicanism, continues its march through history to the delight of royalty buffs throughout the world. Similarly, with the other nine countries in Europe where sovereigns still reign, a substantial segment of the global public follows in the media the royal activities with unabashed curiosity.

Not counting the former kingdoms of Bavaria, Hanover, Serbia, Saxony, Württemberg and the Two Sicilies, the duchies of Parma, Oldenberg and Mecklenburg and the principalities of Anhalt, Baden, Hesse, Lippe-Biesterfeld, Schramburg-Lippe and Montenegro, which were variously incorporated into the imperial realms of Germany and Austro-Hungary and into the kingdoms of Italy and Yugoslavia after World War I, there are, in 2004, fourteen sovereign, previously monarchist countries in continental Europe: Albania, Austria, Bulgaria, France, Georgia, Germany, Greece, Hungary, Italy, Poland, Romania, Russia, Turkey and Yugoslavia that were shorn of their hereditary ruling dynasties relatively recently. In many of these nations, noble titles continue in daily use, socially if not officially. In France, for instance, there are hundreds of noble families, descended from various royal regimes, who are part of the warp and woof of the broader social fabric. In the French Republic, these patricians thread their way through modern society in every province, in every sort of enterprise and profession. In Italy, Germany, Austria – actually in *all* the former monarchies except those previously gripped tightly within the Soviet bloc – bankers, doctors, farmers, diplomats, corporate executives and others with titles of nobility carry on without a royal house in place, but with their own pedigrees happily displayed and socially acknowledged.

Russian, Polish, Hungarian and other Eastern European royal refugees from the Soviet system, have surfaced in their native lands to try to reclaim their hereditary positions or at least to capitalize somehow on their heritage For the most part they are welcomed into the newly democratic societies.

From an historical standpoint Ireland can, of course, be listed among the countries in Europe that were ruled by hereditary monarchies. There is a surprising number of the old ruling Gaelic dynasties whose unbroken lines reach back more than forty generations.

During my almost fifty years of association with Ireland – as a diplomat and as a private resident in County Mayo – I have encountered more than mere traces of the old Celtic royals. Similarly, my colleague Gordon Wetmore, living and painting in County Carlow, has met a number of dynastic families whose ancestors were hereditary rulers. In 2000 we decided to seek out the authenticated descendants of the Irish rulers and to chronicle their links to Ireland's past. The search lasted three years and spread to the United Kingdom, Europe, Africa, Australia, the United States and of course, Ireland.

The family sagas of these dynasts, the current chiefs of the name – stretching over a period of eleven centuries – constitute a history of Ireland itself. These are the stories of the Irish kings from AD 900 to 2004.

# I

# The Old Order

A new horizon for royalty-watching has recently been emerging from the mists of history. In 1944, after decades of research, academic debate and historical soul-searching, Ireland began the official recognition of the hereditary titles of the great Gaelic families. The about-to-be Republic's decision followed intense documentation that had publicly identified the survivors of the royal Gaelic dynasties that, historians agree, are amongst the oldest in Europe.

In 1991 the Standing Council of Irish Chiefs was officially instituted; the President of Ireland, Mary Robinson, bestowing an important protocolary embrace, invited the Council to have its inaugural reception at Áras an Uachtarán, the presidential residence in the Phoenix Park, Dublin. There are only twenty of these noble Irish dynastic families who have survived the turbulent centuries, who maintain their ancient titles and who were now formally acknowledged by the government.

The invasions, occupations, confiscations, rebellions, famines and wars that have swept across the island over the centuries had virtually obliterated the ancient royal dynasties – at least the purely Gaelic-Celtic trappings of them. The Irish, from time immemorial, however, have been ardent genealogists dedicated to preserving the identities and relationships of their families in the face of great opposition, particularly during the invasions by the English and the Normans.

With ever-changing degrees of success, for almost eight hundred years, the English strove to eliminate the dangerous threat of attack by disparate but fierce Gaelic chiefs, whose Celtic culture – including language and religion – alien to Anglo-Saxon-Norman England; it was a periodic but relentlessly violent and mutually bruising process driven by the English urge to expand and colonize. The English Crown was further prodded by its chronic dread of an invasion of Britain by French and/or Spanish (or, in modern times, even German) forces, in alliance with the Irish, possibly striking from several directions. That fear was justified several times in history. But Ireland eventually survived into the modern era as an independent nation.

The island is now politically four-fifths whole: the six counties in Northern Ireland are still partitioned as a part of the United Kingdom; the ancient animosities – referred to by British Foreign Office functionaries as 'the Irish Question', 'the Ulster Problem' or 'the Troubles' – are still alive there, but with a hope of diminished violence and increased co-operation between the historical antagonists. The other twenty-six counties comprise the Republic of Ireland, which was officially created on Easter Monday 1949. In the early 1990s and until 2003, Ireland (or Éire, as the twenty-six counties are sometimes referred to) became one of the most dynamic economies in Europe, producing an unprecedented prosperity referred to admiringly in the world press as the 'Celtic Tiger'.

To subdue a nation, the first essential had been to destroy or render impotent its leadership: the kings, the chiefs, the aristocracy, the spiritual and intellectual powers. Although ultimately abandoned, this strategy – in varying forms and under different reigns – was carried out effectively by the English in Ireland over the centuries: the aristocratic native Irish families were mostly executed, banished into exile, dispossessed and reduced to penury, or, in many cases, married into. The process decimated the hereditary dynastic class that represented the historical Gaelic order from very ancient times. The English were so brutally determined to erase Irish institutions and leadership from history that even the dustbin seemed to have been destroyed. But through the eras of conquest and control, the Irish identity – much of the time camouflaged and furtively sustained – survived, both at home as well as abroad and eventually emerged into the modern era to negotiate its independence as a sovereign state.

J.C. Beckett, Professor of Irish History at Queen's University Belfast, liked to remind students of another aspect of the Gaelic past:

> When they arrived, ancient Gaels surely found Ireland already occupied by a mixture of peoples, the descendants of earlier invaders from Britain and the continent – some of whom most likely spoke a Celtic dialect similar to Gaelic. The Gaels themselves, it is believed, treated the existing population in much the same way as they themselves were treated by later invaders: they killed some, dispossessed some and compelled the rest to pay tribute.

Professor Beckett draws a further parallel to the Anglo-Normans in Ireland:

> Even when the Gaelic conquest was complete – around the fifth century

> AD – the Gaels formed only an ascendancy class, holding the best land and trying to concentrate political power in their hands. They imposed their language and their druidic legal system on the whole country. There were old Gaelic historians and genealogists who had even reconstructed the past so as to obscure the great diversity in the original population.

It would be naïve and inaccurate for observers to over-simplify the dynamics of the long and extremely complex relationship between Ireland and England. Many factors have contributed to this bewilderingly sophisticated tapestry and endless nuances have affected Anglo-Irish history at every level and through every era – including the current one. It has not been purely a saga of conquest and resistance, or even love and hate: it is a multi-faceted symbiotic association both cursed and blessed by history.

The traces of the old Gaelic order can be found by the dedicated seeker. A farmer eking out a desperate living in the wilds of Connemara may have valid and documented bloodlines back to a high king or chief and be infinitely more aristocratic genealogically than the Anglo-Irish gentry living nearby whose family has thrived in recent generations, mainly by the grace of the English ascendancy in Ireland.

In order to find the historical traces of the Gaelic royals, one must combine certain characteristics of the archaeologist, anthropologist, librarian, hiker, sportsman and bon vivant. Also required are a pair of wellingtons, a dinner jacket and black tie, and tolerance for strong spirits – both spectral and liquid. The enticing search for royal traces can be nicely enhanced by an appreciation of William Butler Yeats' concept of the 'Celtic twilight', along with a passing knowledge of pre-medieval and medieval Irish, English, Scottish, Danish, French and Spanish history. Another essential ingredient for a successful effort is time – moments to chat and to reflect on the histories of the old ruling families.

The search for the long-submerged survivors, however, may now have become less daunting than in the past: after World War II reams of information, sequestered by the old families for generations, started to emerge and to be assembled. Research reports, pedigrees and other documentation have been obtained from historical, archeological and genealogical societies, as well as from academic centres – the National University of Ireland, Trinity College Dublin, Oxford and Cambridge Universities, the Royal Irish Academy – and from both public and private sources in France, Spain, Portugal, Austria, Russia, Sweden, the United Kingdom, Australia and North and South America, where thousands of the Irish aristocrats fled long ago and where many of the noble descendants of these ancient Irish families still live today.

The universal fascination with survival has now focused additionally on these few old Gaelic families who, while deeply aware of their own and their peers' bloodlines, have remained generally – in fact, many times purposely – obscure, their genealogical pre-eminence known only to certain scholars and to extended family and community members in their own dynastic regions. Many of the old royalist Catholic families intermarried, for political expediency, with the English/Norman occupiers creating much of the inimitable coterie of 'the Anglo-Irish' who, though a small minority of the island's population, maintained their ascendancy in Irish political and social affairs for six generations and are still prominent on the social and sporting scene in Ireland. A lot of the old Irish dynasts' blood is carried in the veins of this often eccentric, creative, horse-happy, mainly Church of Ireland (Protestant) group.

As the ancient Gaelic royal descendants emerge, with some hesitation, from the shadows of antiquity, the gathering of observers is led by historians and genealogists; but certain to follow are history addicts and match-makers, politicians and tourist boards – and, of course, the general public whose interest, as always, stretches from the merely curious to the fully enthralled.

# II

# The Claimants

Although generally considered a small country, Ireland has, from the beginning of recorded history, been too big to ignore. Its size and position – over 32, 000 square miles located only 500 miles from the coast of France – could not be dismissed strategically; this geographic fact of life made it necessary for England, with its own 50, 000 square miles, to take seriously that neighbouring Gaelic territory just across St George's Channel or the Irish Sea. The various over-lords of England had sparked intrigues and triggered conflicts for centuries with the other contiguous, ethnically different and independent Gaelic realms – the kingdom of the Scots (30,000 sq. miles) and the principality of Wales (8000 sq. miles) – both of which England eventually conquered and put under one Crown: its own. A similar agenda was prepared for Ireland.

The island of Ireland is roughly the same size as modern Austria, only slightly smaller than Portugal and Hungary, twice the size of Denmark, a quarter larger than Belgium, the Netherlands and Luxembourg (Benelux) *combined* and three times bigger than Israel. Along with its land mass and its strategic geographic position, Ireland's population – currently about five million counting all thirty-two counties – was definitely not an insignificant consideration as English policy evolved for over a thousand years.

Historian Joe Lee, Glucksman Professor of Irish Studies at New York University, has pointed out in his lectures that census figures for 1841, just prior to the famines of the mid-nineteenth century, showed there were 8.175 million inhabitants in Ireland – not counting the possible 200,000 evasive purely Irish-speakers along the western seaboard. By 1800, before the Great Famine of 1845–50, the population of Ireland was well over three times that of Scotland and nearly half that of England – a statistic that, at the time, provoked official concern in the United Kingdom. In earlier times, however, there was a recurring circumstance that gave some comfort to prospective invaders of Ireland: the profusion of its Gaelic leaders and the disparities between them.

Celtic-speaking peoples came to Britain and to Ireland from continental Europe about 600 BC. The Gaels themselves – or Goidels – probably reached Ireland during the first century BC, coming directly from Gaul in that vast Celtic area in Europe including modern France, reaching south to the Iberian peninsula of modern Spain and Portugal, east to modern Switzerland and Austria, north to parts of Germany and west to today's English Channel – and eventually across to the British Isles. The Gaels brought sophisticated cultural traditions and expertise, their own root language and a complex tribal legal system (the Brehon Laws). They also transplanted a warrior aristocracy and a well-defined religion (druidism) that prevailed until Christianity was introduced to Ireland in the fifth century by the former slave from Britain, St Patrick.

By the first century AD the Celts were fully established in Ireland. Periodic invasions by the Norse from Scandinavia, as well as by the Welsh, Scots and English, had characterized the earlier eras, but until the Norman invasion in 1170, the pre-eminence of the Celts was not seriously challenged. In fact, many of the Anglo-Norman families settled permanently in Ireland, intermarrying with Celtic families and eventually becoming – as expressed in the historians' weary cliché, 'hiberniores hibernicis ipsis' (more Irish than the Irish themselves). The highly developed Brehon Law functioned right up to the Tudor conquest in the sixteenth century and its influence lingered on for centuries – an enduring frustration for the English colonization process.

In the early centuries of the first millennium Ireland was divided into about 150 units of government, or small kingdoms called *tuath*, an autonomous group of people of independent political jurisdiction under a king. Larger units, comprising several tuath, were built up by local kings whose families maintained their ascendancy traditionally. Some thirty of these larger monarchical units existed by the early twelfth century.

The king (*rí*) of the *tuath* was bound by personal allegiance to a superior king (*ru rí*) who, in turn, was similarly bound to an over-king, 'king of superior kings' (*rí ruirech*) – i.e. the king of a province, the highest ruler recognized in the Brehon Laws. The notion of a king of Ireland to whom *all* the provincial kings owed allegiance, the high-king (*ard rí*) was a later development. (*Rí*, the Irish word for 'king', is from the same root as Hindu *raja*, Latin *rex*, Gaulish *rix,* French *roi* and Spanish *rey*.)

Basically, there were four provincial over-kingdoms: Ulster, Munster, Leinster and Connacht. (The word 'provincial' is misleading since originally they themselves had no superior and each was completely independent on a huge island that had never been a single united country.) Although each over-king was originally autonomous, a special nimbus of mystique seems to have always enhaloed the king whose realm included the sacred Hill of Tara in Meath in Leinster where the ancient Celtic gods had dwelt with the kings and druids since the dawn of history. The dynasty of the king of Tara eventually became the first high kings of Ireland, those ultimate overlords who held the allegiances of the superior over-kings and brought Ireland under one paramount ruler – at least for certain periods and rarely without challenge or opposition in some form. In the various royal families, internecine strife between the aspirants to the high-kingship was a feature of Irish life from the tenth century until the destruction of the old order.

The Irish kings, as well as the nobles and other aristocratic rulers, survived the cascade of historical events by traditionally tight family ties, courage, astute alliances, luck and guile. While the high-kingship was finally overwhelmed by 'foreign' (i.e. mainly English) force and by domestic intrigue, the royals, in a number of instances, kept their provincial and regional sway. The reign of the last high king of Ireland ended in 1152, but the various rui rí and rí held their hereditary positions for generations; in some cases their royal influences were in place as late at the nineteenth century in local areas.

Today, the three senior royal pretenders or claimants – descended from the high-kings in genealogically authenticated lines of legitimacy – are The O'Neill of Clanaboy (Ulster/Leinster), who lives in Setubal, Portugal; The O'Brien, Prince of Thomond (Munster), who lives near Shannon Airport on his ancestral land; and O'Conor Don, Prince of Connacht, who lives in East Sussex, England. They are the respective heads of their own royal houses – i.e. chiefs of the name – as well as co-heirs to Ireland's high-kingship.

A few political scientists and historians in Europe and America believe that these ancient dynasties, which reigned for well over a millennium, could offer Ireland a new (yet old) and interesting national direction. Professor Robert von Dassanowsky of the University of Colorado is one:

> If the country were to return to the high kingship, it could operate on the alternative principal of the past – much as Malaysia operates today – so that each of the three dynasties in turn might provide a sovereign. Also, the fact that the Chiefs of these dynasties are not exclusively Roman Catholic and are genealogically lined to the early English kings might recommend itself to the Northern Ireland Protestants who still assert a monarchist preference in Ireland – albeit an English queen in London.

Whatever the prospects for the old Gaelic royal blood, whatever impact its renaissance would have on the social and economic scenes – if any – a number of scholars are keen to observe its emergence from the shadows of history in the persons of the three legitimate claimants to the Irish high kingship – along with the seventeen chiefs of the name, direct descendants of the other Irish kings, whose genealogical legitimacy has been confirmed.

# III

# The Chiefs

In addition to The O'Brien, O'Conor Don and The O'Neill, who are today the legitimate claimants to the ard rí's crown – the high kingship – and are as well chiefs of the name, there are so far seventeen other Chiefs descended from the ancient kings, superior kings and provincial kings whose genealogies were formally authenticated and whose positions were officially recognized by the Republic and registered in the Office of the Chief Herald. Most members of this group of hereditary dynasts belong to the Standing Council of Irish Chiefs whose current elected chairman is The O'Brien, Lord Inchiquin, Prince of Thomond. Other chiefs of the name are as follows in chronological order of registration with their current locations.

- The MacDermot, Prince of Coolavin, Dec. 1944
  Naas, County Kildare
- The McGillicuddy of the Reeks, Dec. 1944
  Mullingar, County Westmeath
- The O'Callaghan, Dec. 1944
  Barcelona, Spain
- The O'Donoghue of the Glens, Dec. 1944
  Tullamore, County Offaly
- The O'Donovan, Dec. 1944
  Skibbereen, County Cork
- The O'Morchoe (Murphy) of Oulartleigh, Dec. 1944
  Gorey, County Wexford
- The Fox, Dec. 1944
  Mildura, Victoria, Australia
- The O'Grady of Kilballyowen, Dec. 1944
  Sussex, England

- The O'Kelly of Gallagh and Tycooly, Dec. 1944
  Dalkey, County Dublin
- The O' Donnell of Tirconnell, Sept. 1945
  Harare, Zimbabwe
- The MacMorrough Kavanagh, Aug. 1946
  Pembrokeshire, South Wales
- The O' Long of Garranelongy, Aug. 1989
  Faranes, County Cork
- The O' Dogherty (Ó Dochartaigh) of Inishowen, June 1990
  Cadiz, Spain
- The Maguire of Fermanagh, June 1990
  Dublin
- The O'Carroll of Ely, June 1993
  Stockton, California
- The O' Ruairc (O'Rorke) of Breifne, May 1993
  London
- MacDonnell of the Glens, May 1995
  Dublin

Prior to the final suppression of the Brehon system early in the seventeenth century, there were many more chiefs than the scant twenty who were officially recognized and registered by the State and represented by the Standing Council. Additionally, there are some whose credentials are awaiting genealogical decision after lengthy review; some whose centuries-old family records have proven flawed, or at least questionable; and a few whose claims are judged to be lacking merit or, at worst, fraudulent and are now in the Irish Courts of Law.

Recognition of authenticity is taken very seriously by both the applicants and any genuine assessing authority; the criteria are stringent. On occasion, emotions run high – for instance, the case of The MacCarthy Mór, Prince of Desmond, whose registration by the State in 1989 was revoked for reasons of bogus genealogical data: Terence MacCarthy's recognition as chief of the name was made null and void in 1999. Mr MacCarthy, an Eastern Orthodox Christian and formerly one of the most active members of the Standing Council of Chiefs, has mounted a counter-action from his villa in Morocco.

To almost all the chiefs of the name as well as to the Irish government itself, the very antiquity and unbroken continuity of the great Gaelic dynasties justifies rigid protocol in the process of recognition. (For reasons of age and/or apathy a few of the Chiefs register no opinion on the matter.)

Sir Christopher Ewart-Biggs, Her Britannic Majesty's ambassador to Ireland served at the same time as the author served as American ambassador in the mid-1970s. Sir Christopher commented on Ireland's ancient royal traditions during a chat about Irish history in Dublin. He pointed out that in Europe, only the royal Georgian-Armenian family of Bagration-Moukransky comes close to the antiquity of the old Irish royals and are certainly the oldest of the *Christian* dynasties. The early kings of Ireland were Druidic. If a modicum of credit is given to the accuracy of Gaelic oral history, Irish dynasties can be fairly well authenticated back to 200 BC.

(Ambassador Ewart-Biggs relished the Irish and their complex history and had long worked effectively as a diplomat for the cause of Anglo-Irish friendship and peace. It was cruelly ironic that this badly wounded survivor of the Battle of El Alamein in World War II was assassinated in Dublin by a bomb placed by the rogue Provisional Irish Republican Army, in 1976, just two hours after he had discussed with the author some encouraging improvements in Northern Ireland's sectarian violence.)

Heredity and antiquity surely breed dazzling complexity. As bizarre as its survival may seem, the application of the historic Gaelic Brehon Law in matters of succession today has complicated and intensified the process of official recognition of the chiefs. The long shadow of the old Celtic druidic tradition still falls across the decisions regarding the Irish chiefs and seems to be prevailing. One of the most delicate controversies – provoking opposing views even among some of the chiefs themselves – is between those few supporting the more universally applied rule of *primogeniture*, versus the Brehon system of *tanistry*: primogeniture, strictly adhered to in Britain and most other European countries, mandates that the eldest child succeed the incumbent; tanistry, the ancient Gaelic process used in Ireland for nearly a thousand years, requires nomination/election of the noble successor from within a closely defined hereditary group.

While most people would consider such disputes numbingly esoteric, the Standing Council of Chiefs do not share that perspective: matters involving the recognized noble chiefs and those who may eventually be embraced officially are taken seriously – in the interest of Ireland.

The ancient process of succession to the kingship that prevailed through the eras of the Gaelic order was based on a tribal family cluster called the *derbhfine*. Several derbhfine would constitute a *tuath*. The tuath, in turn, were linked together into federations. All Irish kings of whatever rank were either in allegiance to an over-king or they themselves exercised suzerainty over sub-kings.

The derbhfine extended over four generations of a family and the king was chosen from among that group. In effect, anyone whose great-grandfather had been king was theoretically eligible for election – although candidacy was usually confined to one of the three generations of the derbhfine. The head of a family, chiefs of every degree and the king himself were all chosen by an electoral college consisting of the sons, grandsons and even great- grandsons of a common ancestor.

In the old tradition, succession was a combination of the elective with the hereditary principal and was a logical application of the Irish laws of inheritance. Seniority, the basis of primogeniture, was a rejected principle; according to Brehon Law, a king was appointed by virtue of his ancestry, personal ability, accomplishments, military process and intellectual power. The law did not forbid the succession of the eldest son providing he was qualified and had the support of the electoral college.

In the twelfth century the practice of appointing an heir apparent, a *tánaiste* (tanist), while the king or chief still lived, had evolved from custom into a formalized process that survives today. The tanist could – and can – be any qualifying member of the derbhfine. *Tánaiste* means 'second' in Irish, but was originally the past participle of 'expected'. All of the twenty currently recognized chiefs of the name have their duly identified tanists.

Primogeniture came to Ireland with the English and the Normans and, as the force of their power extended, so did the principle of seniority in matters of inheritance. Even by the early centuries of the first millennium, primogeniture had come to be accepted as the normal form of succession in several regions of Ireland – as well as among many old Irish families who had married into the ascendant noble families of the invaders (and vice versa), or had accepted Anglo-Norman grants and titles in exchange for fealty. English custom and law had become so compelling in certain provinces, in fact, that the Irish kings themselves attempted to introduce primogeniture; they were, however, consistently foiled by the insistence of the derbhfine on their traditional rights.

The entrenched power of the derbhfine and tanistry against the right of the English primogeniture laws created unforeseen strife and havoc and produced arguments that persist today; when the ancient Gaelic way of governance came in contact with Anglo-Norman feudalism the friction was explosive. Dublin historian Eoin MacNeill considered this (confrontation) the rock on which Henry III's scheme to bring the native Irish lords to civility would founder.

It was impossible for the invaders to bring Ireland into submission without eliminating the Gaelic social order and the system of law that gave it strength – laws that reflected a totally different social concept and philosophy of life. Extremely significant in this clash between Irish and English politics were the different successional laws and the special constraints put upon an Irish ruler: in England the monarch was paramount; in Ireland, the ultimate power resided in the derbhfine.

The Brehon purists, the Gaelic traditionalists, recoiled from the principle of primogeniture in the matters of succession and inheritance. As the English ascendancy in Ireland expanded and the old Gaelic order receded over the centuries into regional isolation and marginal consequence, primogeniture pushed aside the derbhfine electoral system as the dominant process.

The Gaelic tradition, however, endures: it survives today with respect, understanding and a pertinence limited (at the moment) to specific cases of inheritance and, significantly, to the Standing Council where, even there, opinions on the matter are sometimes at variance. Although many of the old dynastic families have for centuries accepted the newer, imported process of primogeniture that was accompanied by English domination and enforcement of English law, the majority of the individual chiefs now support the ancient Gaelic system of aristocratic election and tanistry; they consider the old Gaelic system persuasively appropriate in matters relating to succession among the Gaelic chiefs of the name.

The complexities of the procedure for recognition of the legitimate line of descendants of the ancient aristocrats are increased by the fact that a number of the princely Gaelic families reside outside Ireland, are not Irish – by nationality – and have not been for many generations. A few others are Irish nationals who live and work abroad and several are British subjects. A widespread but inaccurate view holds that the only noteworthy diaspora of the Irish occurred during the Great Famines of the 1840s and 1850s when most of those fleeing the tragic circumstances of the island headed west to North America. In the seventeenth and eighteenth centuries, however, aside from individual cases of emigration for reasons of religious persecution, ambition, debts, blood feuds, or even for romance and adventure, there were other exoduses, the most notable and longest-lasting one being the lyrically named 'Flight of the Wild Geese'.

The main body of the Wild Geese were Irish Jacobites, supporters of James II, the Stuart Catholic King of England, Scotland and Ireland, who, with his loyal Irish and Old English followers, was defeated and forced to abdicate, fleeing to exile in France in 1691 six years after inheriting the crown from his brother Charles II. The Jacobites – civilians along with the royalist Irish troops and officers – faced ruin and execution by remaining at home in Ireland. This pressure to escape to the Continent was powerful and persistent and the Irish diaspora to France and to other European countries was unusual in its scale and duration: between the Treaty of Limerick in 1691 following James II's defeat and the Treaty of Aix-la-Chapelle in 1748 between Britain, France, Holland, Germany, Spain and Genoa, more than fifty thousand Irish – a large number by eighteenth century standards – fled to mainland Europe, principally to France, which had been resolutely sympathetic to the Stuart dynasty. They fled also in significant numbers to

Austria, Spain, Germany and Russia. The greater part of the Catholic gentry of Ireland departed into exile at the defeat of their Stuart king at the hands of his Protestant Dutch son-in-law, Prince William of Orange.

These Wild Geese of noble descent had ranking positions in the military, commercial and intellectual echelons of Irish society. Their support of the Catholic Stuart Crown made them compatible additions to the royalist French establishment within which many of these Irish emigré families and their descendants eventually achieved wealth and prominence – such as Edme Patric Maurice MacMahon, who was a French marshal, the first Duc de Magenta and became president of France in 1873. Others became prime ministers of Spain (two) and Austria (three).

For twelve years the exiled monarch, James II, lived with his family and an expanding number of Jacobite hangers-on in Saint-Germaine-en-Laye, a village about ten miles west of Paris. The royal Stuart court, operating in delusional splendour and nourished by expectancy, was protected by their deposed sovereign's cousin, King Louis XIV. The Jacobites and their cause (i.e. a Stuart Restoration) were given asylum along with military assurances and financial support against the rival Tudors until a Stuart could be triumphantly returned to the throne of England. Scores of Irish officers among the Jacobites fought in French and other European royalist armies for the common cause of Britain's defeat. The Stuarts' prospects then evaporated with the Treaty of Aix-la-Chapelle, which ended the hostilities and declared that no Pretenders to the English throne could reside within any of the countries that were signatories to it.

In these continental armies many of the Irish aristocrats were knighted for services to the exiled Stuarts and to the reigning Bourbons. In France, to be accepted at court – and even into their officer corps – the Irish refugees had to show evidence that their family was of ancient or noble origin. This usually presented no problem since the old Gaelic tradition of keeping meticulous genealogies was strongly held amongst the Wild Geese.

Contrary to the more romantic historical accounts, the Wild Geese were not comprised exclusively of nobles, gentry and the scions of the great Gaelic families; they included sons from every social class. Nor was the Wild Geese's flight for purely political reasons as supposed. While the defeat of the Jacobite cause in Ireland was the main catalyst, the Wild Geese also constituted a mercantile migration. As the first became settled, others followed with families and entourage of all aspects.

The Flight of the Wild Geese is often confused with the 'Flight of the Earls', another crucial event at the beginning of the seventeenth century. After the bloody campaigns in various sectors of the island, the English finally broke the back of Irish resistance – for a period – at the strategic Battle of Kinsale in County Cork in 1601. This earlier devastating defeat forced two of the most powerful representatives of the Gaelic princely families to flee certain execution: Hugh O'Neill, the Earl of Tyrone and his peer and ally, Rory O'Donnell, Earl of Tirconnell – direct ancestors of the current chiefs of the name. These formerly all powerful Catholic lords of northern Ireland whose families had fought the invasions and colonization of a succession of English crowns for generations, finally gathered a small band of about one hundred men, women and children and fled abroad – in a boat brought secretly into Lough Swilly in Donegal – into the protection of the French and Austrian royal courts as fellow enemies of the English.

The Flight of the Earls is commonly seen by historians to mark the end of Gaelic Catholic Ulster and to have opened the way for the huge Anglo-Scottish plantation of Northern Ireland. This strategy was designed to secure enduring English dominance over the defeated Catholic power in the region by transplanting an anti-Catholic populace onto the land of the dispossessed Irish farmers, gentry and nobles: lowland Scot Presbyterians were pressured by the English to shift from their historical homelands along the England-Scotland border, as well as from the Highlands, to the alien Irish turf across St George's Channel. It was a process calculated to tilt the balance of regional power. The results of this plantation are reflected today in the animosity between extremists in the Catholic and Presbyterian communities in Northern Ireland.

During his four-year posting as American ambassador in Paris from 1989 to 1993, the author became a close friend of the Irish ambassador to France, John Campbell. Campbell, who later headed Ireland's Permanent Mission to the United Nations in New York and, in 1998, became ambassador to Spain, was intrigued by and knowledgeable about the long Franco-Irish connections – and the history of the Wild Geese. In discussing the subject, Ambassador Campbell often referred to Renagh Holohan, a journalist with *The Irish Times* in Dublin, who, with Jeremy Williams, author and founder of the Irish Victorian Society, had written in 1989 a book called *The Irish Chateaux: In Search of Descendants of the Wild Geese,* which describes sixty castles and a dozen other private residences belonging to the families or relatives of those refugees who left their homeland three centuries ago.

The author called on several of these families whose chateaux and circumstances ranged from splendid to spartan. As Holohan and Williams had observed, these descendants of the sons and daughters of Irish gentry – although now French in all but name – retain a strong interest in their backgrounds. They all proudly displayed their genealogies and were happy to recount their families' stories; about half spoke English and two patriarchs even had a passing knowledge of the Irish language.

'Strangely, they are almost as out of step with modern France as they are with modern Ireland', Holohan wrote. "'Ancien régime" in attitude, they are almost all solidly royalist and universally refer to the so-called Old Pretender (James III *de jure*, son of King James II, their ancestors' Stuart leader and benefactor), as "Jacques Trois" and in many cases they have named their sons "Charles Edouard" after Bonny Prince Charlie, the Young Pretender. Their view of Ireland is decidedly anachronistic: wholly Catholic, "Celtic" and, in a historical dimension, anti-English.'

Three of the 'Irish chateaux' have links to current chiefs of the name and descendants of the high-kings: O'Conor in northern France, O'Kelly in the Loire Valley, O'Neill in Paris and its environs and O'Brien in Nantes.

The adapting of the Brehon Law to today's world and the complications arising from the foreign birth and residence of some for the old Irish aristocratic families – the Wild Geese being an important but only one example – have re-enforced the formality of the process of official recognition. In 1999 The O'Brien, Prince of Thomond, as a member and executive of the Standing Council, commented privately on the twenty existing recognitions and advised that there were several more applications being reviewed. He confirmed that the process was tedious – but thorough. There are no newly elected chiefs, he explained: it is a matter of identifying the old title and its linkage to the present and of establishing the integrity of the genealogical documentation. Sometimes it is all in hand except for one piece, one missing link, but without it, the process ceases.

With regard to the incidences of deliberate falsification or other ruses involved in the recognition process, Conor O'Brien remarked that there had been several interesting – and even astonishing – cases of well-known family names being singed in the procedure: the majority of the applications are, of course, totally straightforward. Every now and then, however, there is the rare excitement and ultimate sadness of hoax – some of which are impressively elaborate and clever. The procedure must be painstaking because the accuracy of the nation's history is fundamentally at stake.

❧

In May 1999, the author visited Brendan O'Donoghue, the Chief Herald of Ireland, in the Genealogical Office whose headquarters are on the top floor of the National Library in Dublin. For bureaucratic reasons the office had been moved several years previously from its traditional location in Dublin Castle, for generations the executive epicentre of the English ascendancy-dominated government. O'Donoghue described the rationale and the logic involved in the official recognition of the titles relating to the descendants of the great princely families; while citing the twenty recognized incumbent chiefs of the name – including, of course, the three ard-rí descendants – he mentioned two others that were currently under review.

There are, of course, many other families of (predominantly) Gaelic royal blood, Brendan O'Donoghue noted, but whose proof of the genealogical line back to the ancient monarchs was flawed in some way; certain documents were simply missing. Also, he stressed, at times the family's process of inheritance in modern times had been questioned by both the Chief Herald's office and by the Standing Council of Chiefs who might have contrary views on the credentials: here once again was the enduring collision between the 'first-born' principle of primogeniture and the derbhfine electoral process mandated by Brehon Law.

The first Chief Herald of Ireland, Edward MacLysaght, commented officially on the differing views many years ago:

> The Genealogical Office has encountered some opposition from a few historians and Celtic scholars on the grounds that to determine a Chieftainry by primogeniture was a departure from the principles of the Gaelic-Irish system. We argued – and were generally supported in this – that to reject primogeniture would result in taking no action at all in the matters and that, furthermore, at the end of the Gaelic period, the succession had been, in most cases, by primogeniture (anyway) …

The logic of those with an opposing view in this debate is equally simple: why should primogeniture – imposed in Ireland by a foreign power – be accepted today as the proper legal process in determining inheritance within the Gaelic social order that the foreign invaders had officially abolished and destroyed so many centuries ago?

There does not seem to be any vindictiveness involved when the old traditional policy prevails; it is, the derbhfine purists maintain, strictly a matter of logic and legitimacy (with, perhaps understandably, just a hint of relish lurking in the hearts of a few Gaelic scholars for this morsel of historical retribution).

Most of the officially unrecognized princely descendants are acknowledged within their own extended Gaelic families and friends and their ancient lineage is also respected within their particular historic regions. Many others of the great families, who are not included on the official list for whatever reason, have been long gone from the specific areas of their ancestral prominence, but are well known in the broader social circles of Ireland and abroad.

Will these descendants of the old Irish rulers, the royal survivors, become (or remain) custodians of a Proustian dream of past glory, men who merely provide an interesting texture to the vibrant social fabric of the country? Or will the bearers of the old Gaelic royal blood, whose legacies have been hidden by and from history for so long, emerge into a twenty-first century Ireland that recognizes their linkage to Ireland's ancient monarchical system? In the stories that follow, these are the authenticated descendants of the Irish royals, the mostly hidden dynasts of today whose families have miraculously escaped the dustbin of history and who are now entering their second and even third millennium of traceable nobility.

# IV

# The Past and the Future

Even in modern Ireland, a sophisticated participant on the world political stage, one is consistently reminded of history's persistent grip on the present. And if the past is prologue, history will have an enormous effect on Ireland's future; this linkage of past and future will influence dramatically the lives of the emerging tradition-based Irish royal lines. One of the darker legacies of the past is the widespread ignorance of Ireland's history: there is a surprising lack of basic knowledge on that subject, for example, in the United States where over thirty-three million citizens are of Irish extraction. This absence of information – combined with ingrained misconceptions about Ireland – seems almost pervasive and crosses all social and political lines.

At almost any dinner party in a city or suburb in North America virtually any question regarding the facts about Ireland, historical or current, (e.g. Who is the president? What is the population?) would most likely be met either by startling inaccuracies or a chilling blank on most faces at the table.

The same syndrome applies to the tightly-knit Irish-American urban communities comprised mainly of second and third generation Americans, some of whom have never been to Ireland, but have loyally supported the Irish Republican Army's violence-prone political position. They love and (feel that they) know 'the old country'. Specific questions, however, about Ireland and its history often produce the familiar glaze over a surprising number of eyes in these communities of Irish-descended Americans.

The late Ambassador Christopher Ewart-Biggs – who was very familiar, personally and professionally, with the United States – once proclaimed, with a wink, that he had finally identified the Ultimate American Bore: it is, he said, the person who, when Ireland is mentioned, gushes patronizingly about his or her affection for the Irish that was instilled in childhood by the nanny from Donegal and/or by the family's Irish housemaids. It often turns out,

Ewart-Biggs declared, that the family's domestic staff was as fictitious as the person's knowledge of Ireland.

Runners-up in the boredom sweepstakes, he added, could be those who actually have visited Ireland, occasionally or even repeatedly and gain their perceptions exclusively through the prism of the lingering English ascendancy's optic.

In an entirely different category of distortion are those whose viewpoints are pre-packaged by Hollywood and Broadway and who see Ireland as a tragic, beautiful, 99.99 per cent Roman Catholic Shangri-la populated by leprechauns, ghosts, bewhiskered aphorists and romantic gun-running tenors, where the farm lads' dream is to marry a raven-haired, nymphomaniac colleen whose father owns a pub near a racetrack.

Americans certainly do not have a monopoly on the lack of understanding about Ireland. Winston Churchill told American Ambassador Lewis Douglas in the 1950s that Britain's 'vast ignorance on the subject of Ireland was a self-inflicted wound'. Foreign policy analysts in the United States, France, Germany and in Britain itself, have pointed out for decades that such broad ignorance – 'hibernia incognita' – in the United States is both anachronistic and dangerous. The 3600 dead, plus the 11,000 casualties, between 1969-2000 due directly to the sectarian violence in Northern Ireland (population 1.5 million), provide support for that warning.

Desmond Guinness of Leixlip Castle in County Kildare, founder and former Chairman of the Irish Georgian Society, lectures in many countries, including the United States, on the subject of Ireland's cultural heritage – particularly its architecturally distinguished demesnes and great houses. Charitably and realistically, Guinness believes that knowledge and proper understanding of Ireland were also casualties of history; people today, he says, should not be unfairly blamed for not knowing about things that were purposely destroyed by or denied to their predecessors.

While it is impossible to reverse the ravages of history, Desmond Guinness feels that it is not too late to educate, to correct the distortions and to make people aware of the extraordinary cultural and intellectual accomplishments of the past: It is a terrible shame, he says, that many Irish – as well as the rest of the world – are not at all familiar with the very productive and creative aristocratic tradition that thrived, at times pre-eminently, in Ireland for centuries.

Guinness and his colleague, Desmond FitzGerald, Knight of Glin, President of the Irish Georgian Society, are missionaries of a sort; they say that their purpose is to bring illumination to areas where light was banished many centuries ago. They seek wider awareness of the artistic and technical creativity, the vast wealth of knowledge, poetry, legends, writing and the great centres of learning that flourished in Ireland in the age of the old monarchs.

In the current era of swift communication, the past may be forced to release its grip of ignorance and neglect. The very existence of Ireland's ancient aristocratic legacy is, it seems, finally being realized by an increasing number of people everywhere – including in Ireland itself. Irish scholars and students of government are examining the past in a new light and are developing long-neglected respect for the ancient Gaelic traditions and the princely dynasties that fostered them. The future, deeply influenced by its Celtic past, has arrived.

# V

# The Royal Survivors

# ULSTER

HUGO O'NEILL

# The O'Neill

## PRINCE OF CLANABOY

While there are numerous O'Neills of aristocratic and noble pedigrees, only two occupy the highest echelon in the royal House of O'Neill. Both are now in their sixties, both are married to women who have their own family titles, both have more than four children and both families have lived for generations in separate countries outside the Republic of Ireland; they speak different languages and have non-Irish passports.

In the matter of a claimant to the hypothetical throne of Ireland, however, only one is acknowledged as the legitimate pretender as well as chief of the name: Hugo The O'Neill, Prince of Clanaboy, who lives in Portugal. Edged out of the top designation by a genealogical quirk in the fifteenth century (which has been calmly debated ever since) is Hugo's distant cousin, Don Carlos O'Neill y Castillo, Marqués de la Granja y del Norte y de Villaverda de San Isidro, Conde de Benagiar, O'Neill Mór, who lives in Spain.

The O'Neills of Ulster have been occupying top levels for a very long time. *Burke's Peerage*, which devotes over twenty thousand words to the O'Neill family listing, says: 'The great dynastic House of O'Neill is the most famous branch of the royal family of Tara, seat of the High Kings, whose recorded filiation is accepted by scholars from about AD 360 and which is the oldest traceable family in Europe.' This conflicts with the O'Conor's ancestral traceability, which goes back to AD 75. (The Georgian/Armenian House of Bagration-Moukransky is probably the oldest of the Christian dynasties. The O'Conor, O'Neill and O'Brien kings of Ireland were pagan before St Patrick started his mission of conversion in the fifth century.)

The O'Neill is the descendant of the legendary, heroic King Niall of the Nine Hostages, who lived fifteen hundred years ago and exerted at least nominal sovereignty over the whole island of Ireland. (The O'Conors and the O'Neills descend from the same forefather – Eochu Mugmaedon who married first Mongfinn, a Munster princess and by her had Brian, ancestor of the O'Conor Don. He married secondly Carina, a Briton princess by whom he had Niall Noígiallach [of the Nine Hostages] who succeeded him as High King of Tara). More historically in focus and quite shorn of legend is King Donell O'Neill, the first of the sept to bear the surname O'Neill, whose eponymous grandfather, Niall, was killed in battle with the Norsemen (Vikings) in AD 919.

The O'Neill sept provided High Kings until the thirteenth century; they subsequently reigned as provincial kings in Ulster until the seventeenth century. Their 'proprietary turf' was, from ancient times, Tír Eoghan (Land of King Eoghan/Owen, the son of Niall of the Nine Hostages) now called Tyrone, which comprised not only that present-day county but most of Derry and Donegal – an extensive realm comparable in size to modern Holland. Eoghan/Owen was the first king of the Úi Neill to be christened by St Patrick – in AD 442 at the Grianán Aileach, a prehistoric round fortress that still stands.

Ulster – which now includes, predominantly, the six British-occupied counties of Northern Ireland, along with Donegal, the Republic's most northern county – was 'O'Neill Country' for virtually a millennium. The O'Neills, along with their powerful allies, the O'Donnells, had an enduring hereditary hegemony that the English found extremely difficult to crack. The O'Neills became accustomed to being in charge and doing it well.

The O'Neills were in command of their own dynastic destinies for over forty generations. As Norman and Anglo-Norman power alternately oozed and coursed into the old Gaelic order and into control, the Irish resistance to it similarly stiffened, eased and again stiffened. The unremitting attempts made by the English in the sixteenth century to exterminate the Irish aristocracy were carried out with a ferocity and perfidy seldom equalled even in that violent age. By the 1600s the invader's grip had tightened and Ulster, the powerful O'Neill province, became the last bastion of opposition and the sole realistic threat to English dominance. Gaelic Ireland's hopes lay in Ulster. The O'Neills themselves had both suffered and profited from English strategy. The policy of surrender and regrant, under which changes in the power structure were carried out, was a compromise arrangement to meet the political difficulties created by the fact that the Irish lords, from the royal O'Neills down to the lesser nobles, held their ancestral lands in defiance of English law and of the nominal English proprietors – notably the Crown. The new policy converted their traditional (Brehon) elective lordships into hereditary estates, granted them English titles and ennobled them with peerages. Conn The O'Neill became Earl of Tyrone, Hugh O'Donnell was made Earl of Tirconnell. (Donal The O'Brien in Connacht was created Earl of Thomond.)

Within a decade of their ennoblement, however, O'Neill and O'Donnell – frustrated and angered by the new arrangements and spurred on by equally furious fellow Irish lords – rebelled violently. Irish forces were raised and serious battle against the English ascendancy was again set in motion.

The O'Neills and the O'Donnells prevailed in the north and north-west of Ireland against the English forces sent by London's government in Dublin and moved to rally allies throughout the island. The Irish lords of the north had been fighting since the mid-1500s to uphold their sovereignty and to keep the English out of the province. The struggle was called 'the Ulster War', which lasted from 1593-1602.

The grandson of Conn the Lame, first Earl of Tyrone, Hugh O'Neill, was the second Earl. Before Conn's death, Shane O'Neill the Proud slew his half-brother Matthew, the first Baron Dungannon who was Hugh O'Neill's father. Hugh, the principal adversary of the Crown, knew that Queen Elizabeth would never agree to a separate solution for Ulster and consequently tried, with surprising success, to involve the whole country in the war to oust the English invaders. In 1598 the O'Neill-led forces had a resounding victory in Tyrone against the enemy's numerically superior and seasoned troops. Hopes for a Gaelic resurgence raced through the Irish countryside like a flame.

Spanish troops, sent by King Philip III of Spain at the Earl of Tyrone's request, arrived by ship at Kinsale on the south coast in support of the Irish armies' fight against Deputy Lord Mountjoy's re-enforced English forces. Attacks, counter-attacks – by land and by sea – led to heightened desperation and demanded the utmost from both sides. The crucial military and historical moment was at hand; it was the final contest that would decide not only the fate of the Irish lords and their loyal followers, but, basically, the future of Gaelic institutions. It would complete – or make possible to complete – the Tudor conquest.

The Irish, even with the Spanish naval and military support – but frustrated by bad weather and poor timing at sea – were soundly defeated at Kinsale. The war ended with The O'Neill's submission in 1603. The dreams of reclaimed Irish sovereignties evaporated. In 1968 Dr G.A. Hayes-McCoy,

Professor of History at University College Galway, recalled, in a lecture in Dublin, the stunning finality of the moment:

> The battle of Kinsale had decided everything. Mountjoy's victory meant the repulse of the essential Spanish invasion and the ultimate overthrow of O'Neill and his forces. It meant also the downfall of the last of the Gaelic lordships and the end of the old Irish world. Queen Elizabeth was dead by the time ofThe O'Neill's surrender, but the policy of her house, the Tudors, had succeeded. Ireland – despite the resistance of so many of her lords – was conquered.
>
> By the early part of the seventeenth century Ulster itself was overrun; the earls had gone: The O'Neill and The O'Donnell – former keepers-of-the-Gaelic-flame as well as the sword – had fled to exile in Europe, after the Battle of Kinsale in 1601, along with scores of their followers: 'The Flight of the Earls'.

Decades later the ancestors of Hugo, the current O'Neill, Prince of Clanaboy, also fought for the cause of the Catholic King James II – at home in Ireland (including at the fateful battle of Kinsale) and abroad – as officers in the Irish Brigade of the French army. Hugo's great-grandfather, Sean (Joâo) O'Neill moved from Dublin to Portugal in 1740 after his father, Black Phelim O'Neill, a Jacobite colonel, was killed while fighting against the English at Malplaquet, France. Joâo settled in Setubal near Lisbon. Hugo and his wife, Rosa Maria, heiress of the Valenca family, premier marques of Portugal, now live on the same O'Neill estate, 'Quintas las Machadas', where his predecessors entertained King Joâo VI, King Ferdinando, King Pedro V and King Luis I, successive reigning sovereigns of Portugal. King Joâo was the incumbent Chief's paternal grandmother's great-grandfather.

Hugo The O'Neill, born (1939) and educated in Lisbon and Rosa Maria have an active social life in the Portuguese capital and at home at Machadas; they move in the highest levels of Lisbon and international society. They are a vibrant, attractive couple who obviously cherish the historical significance and comfortable elegance of their chateau. Although a long–established Portuguese aristocrat, The O'Neill also takes seriously his family's role in Irish history – and his position as a Gaelic royal.

Hugo's father, Jorge (b. 1908), a former admiral in the Portuguese navy, was officially recognized as Chief two decades ago by the Chief Herald of Ireland; he presided at the first international gathering of Clan O'Neill at Shane's Castle in Country Antrim in Northern Ireland in 1982. Jorge died in 1990 and, through the process of Brehon Law (and coincidental primogeniture), Hugo succeeded to the title as The O'Neill of Clanaboy: he was inaugurated as chief of the name in 1992 at Grianán Aileach.

The O'Neill is a successful businessman and investor; he was the chief executive officer of a manufacturing conglomerate for thirty years and now, with his son and tanist, Jorge Maria Empis O'Neill (b. 1970), he heads his own financial consulting firm.

There is no apparent dynastic animosity (regarding the succession) between Hugo and his Spanish kinsman, Don Carlos O'Neill y Castillo, Marqués de la Granja, etc. who lives with his wife, Dona Maria Licenciado, Maestrante de la Real de Silla and their six children on the family estate in Seville. Don Carlos – whose direct ancestors descend from Aeodh, son of Eoghan O'Neill Mór (1432-55) and took the style of O'Neill of the Fews, a territory in Armagh) – prefers not to pursue actively the centuries old genealogical point of dispute over the ancient Gaelic title.

Nor is there any ill-feeling between Hugo, the chief of the name in Setubal and his Ireland-based British cousin, Lord Raymond Arthur Clanaboy O'Neill, 4th Baron O'Neill of Shane's Castle (b. 1933), in County Antrim. Were it not for a female-descended ancestor (not accepted by Brehon Law) and an ensuing change of surname, Raymond might also have been a candidate for succession to the chieftaincy – and to claimancy to the high kingship.

Genealogical complications aside, the O'Neills are traditionally comfortable in commanding positions: Raymond O'Neill's uncle, Captain Terence O'Neill, Lord O'Neill of the Maine, was Prime Minister of Northern Ireland in the 1960s – and was succeeded in the same post by his cousin, James Chichester-Clarke, descendent of English settlers in Ulster.

Hugo The O'Neill visits his Irish cousins every few years; the Portuguese and Irish *joi de vivre* are synergistic; they all have a good time together. Hugo, perhaps predictably, also has his own strongly conservative perspective: he does not view monarchists, nobles and aristocrats as historical dross or echoes from a forgotten Gaelic past; far from it. After his father's death, Hugo even suggested in a letter to American Senator George Mitchell, during the Northern Ireland peace process negotiations, that a re-instated O'Neill dynasty should head an independent Ulster – re-structured as a constitutional monarchy. The senator did not reply.

Hugo feels that all the dispossessed Irish aristocrats, like his own family – i.e. descendants of the Wild Geese – should be provided with Irish passports and that all the officially recognized heads of the old yet enduring Gaelic aristocratic families should sit in the Irish Senate.

Hugo, the chief of the name, is not casual in this attitude. He is a pragmatic and considerate man of affairs, a cultured, scholarly observer of life, and an historian. He says that his opinions come from his mind as well as his heart. As The O'Neill, Prince of Clanaboy and as pretender to the empty throne of Ireland, Hugo's special lineage and its contemporary pertinence will not be easily ignored. This Irish-Portuguese aristocrat will try to make certain of that.

SHANE'S CASTLE, CO. ANTRIM
Engraving after Ashford, 1793; Irish Architectural Archive

DR DON RAMON O'DOGHERTY

# The O'Dogherty

## OF INISHOWEN

The peninsula of Inishowen in Donegal, jutting into the Atlantic Ocean and flanked on its east and west coasts by Lough Foyle and Lough Swilly, lies in the most northern part of the Republic of Ireland; it is the furthest point of the ancestral territory of the Ó Dochartaighs (anglicized variations include O'Dogherty, O'Dougherty, Doherty, Docherty, Dougherty) who have occupied this strategic land mass since the mythic eras of history. Their current chief of the name, however, The O'Dogherty, hereditary Lord of Inishowen (Inis Eóghain/Owen's Island), Dr Don Ramon O'Dogherty, lives in Cadiz in the southern-most region of the kingdom of Spain where members of his branch of the family sought sanctuary and a new life in the seventeenth century.

The sagas of the O'Doghertys, in both Ireland and Spain, are closely representative of the large numbers of Gaelic aristocrats who lost 'the kingdom, the power and the glory' in their own realms, but reacquired portions of each in another one abroad. Furthermore, the O'Doghertys and a lesser number of the ruling Gaelic families were able to retain, through centuries of chaos and upheaval, their genealogical authenticity reaching back for more than twenty-five generations to the kings of Ulster in the fifth century.

The fortunes of the O'Doghertys in the sixteenth, seventeenth and eighteenth centuries were also strikingly similar to those of the other dynastic Irish families; indeed, the fluctuations in position and power reflected the broader aspects of the ever complex Anglo-Irish relationship, that intricate dance of death that went on for centuries: violence followed by embrace followed by violence followed by embrace – a disturbingly familiar two-step in modern Ulster where lethal sectarian strike and a glacier–like peace process co-exist.

Dr Ramon O'Dogherty's great-great-great-great-great-grandfather, Seán

Mór The Ó Dochartaigh of Inishowen, surrendered his chiefly position and power to King Henry VIII and was knighted by the Tudor king in 1541. Seán Mór's grandson (and successor as The Ó Dochartaigh), Seán Óg, rebelled against Queen Elizabeth I, then surrendered and, forty years after his father, was similarly knighted by his former adversaries. As the pendulum swung predictably in the other direction a few years later, Seán Óg was imprisoned by the English for giving aid to the Queen's enemy – in this case, to the survivors of the Spanish Armada, which had been wrecked by fierce storms on the northern coast of Donegal. The devilish two-step has never stopped.

Seán Óg's successor, Caothaoir Ruadh (Red Cahir) Ó Dochartaigh, personified even more luridly the mercurial intercourse between the invaders and the ancient ruling families of Ireland.

Awarded a knighthood by the English before he was twenty, Sir Cahir, a handsome young leader, was lionized in court circles in London and honoured by the Anglo-Irish authorities in Dublin and in Ulster. However, in 1600, appaled and infuriated by a vicious English move of force against members of his Ó Dochartaigh kin, Sir Cahir rebelled in equal force, leading and prompting bloody attacks and counter attacks, sieges, reprisals and battles for expulsion that raged over the northern territories of Donegal, Derry and Tyrone. At the time of the Flight of the Earls in the early 1600s, Sir Cahir was the last of the ruling Gaelic dynasts in Ulster to stand against the English tide of conquest.

Pursued relentlessly as outlaws for several years by thousands of English troops that had been sent expressly to Donegal, in 1608 Sir Cahir and his Ó Dochartaigh militias were ultimately ambushed and wantonly slaughtered at Doon near Kilmacrean between Letterkenny and Milford. Cahir's body was put on public display in Dublin. His severed head was fixed atop a pike at Newgate in London and later returned to Dublin where it was on view at St Auden's Church until 1959. His extensive estates – including, among the vast properties, Culmore Castle on the island of Doagh in Lough Foyle and Burt Castle near Lough Swilly – were seized by Sir Arthur Chichester, the English Lord Deputy of Derry, for his personal property. Six thousand freeholders and tenants, kith and kin of The Ó Dochartaigh, were evicted from the Chief's land and transported to military or other service.

Sir Cahir The Ó Dochartaigh, had died an English baron and an Irish lord. His sword and scabbard – trophies of victory at the time of his beheading – were recovered in a private home in Sligo a hundred years ago and are now on display in the O' Dogherty Castle Museum in Derry.

At the Restoration of King Charles II, Sir Cahir's successor as chief and lord of Inishowen was another Cahir Ó Dochartaigh (1639-1714) who received some compensatory land in Cavan after the earlier confiscation of

Inishowen and became an officer in King James II's army in Ireland. Upon the crushing defeat of the Jacobites and the Stuart cause, Cahir – by then known as Major The O'Dogherty fled with his unit – first to France and soon afterward to Spain. As an Irish noble, he was received warmly by the royal court and became a Lieutenant General in the Spanish army.

One hundred and fifty years later the O'Doghertys in Ireland sought refuge again in Spain. Three of General O'Dogherty's great-grandsons – their lives as Irish gentlemen reduced to utter hopelessness by the severity of the Penal Laws against Roman Catholics – fled their homeland and as their predecessors had done, became officers in the historically elite Royal Spanish Navy. Two of the brothers died as heroes in separate battles at sea; the third, John, had a distinguished combat record as a naval commander in the Napoleonic wars against the French. John was Dr Ramon O'Dogherty's great-grandfather.

For several generations Spain was a most logical destination for the O'Doghertys and many other Irishmen of noble rank who became outlaws in their own land, or refugees in another; Spain's Catholicism and her shared enmity against England created an ideal sanctuary for the fleeing Gaelic aristocrats. The Spanish military and naval services also served well as professional havens for hundreds of displaced Irish gentlemen and their charges. The officer ranks of the Spanish navy, with its aristocratic tradition and excellent historical record, were mutually attractive to many of the highly educated, well bred exiles from the various provinces of Ireland who could not only find a new life, but could, as well, actively seek revenge against the Common Enemy: an independent Ireland in alliance with Spain would threaten the entire structure of English power – based as it was on command of the sea.

Ramon O'Dogherty's grandfather Ramon (1835-1902) and his father, Pascual (1886-1964), followed their immediate predecessors and became Spanish naval officers. Don Pascual O'Dogherty was a distinguished scholar and benefactor of San Fernando where there is a street named in his honour.

The current O'Dogherty, who was born in 1919 in San Fernando, chose a medical career and took his degrees at the Universities of Cadiz and Madrid. Specializing in biopathology, Don Ramon is a member of the Royal Academies of Medicine of Palma de Mallorca, of San Romualdo of Letters, Arts and Sciences and is a member of the Supreme Committee of the Knights Hospitaller of St John the Baptist.

In 1990 Don Ramon was officially recognized by the Office of the Chief Herald in Dublin as chief of the name and clan that includes 300,000 members in Ireland, the United Kingdom, the United States, Canada, Australia, Spain, Argentina and Mexico.

The O'Dogherty and his wife Catalina Fabra, a Lady Hospitaller of St John, have three children, Cristina, Begoña and his tanist, Ramon, a lawyer who lives and works in Seville.

Don Ramon's sisters and brothers have also kept up the O'Dogherty affiliations with Spanish academe and military-naval service begun by Lieutenant General Cahir O'Dogherty in the seventeenth century: the Chief's sisters – Concha, Tany, Maria-Carmen and Bely are college professors; his brother Rear Admiral Pascual O'Dogherty, born in 1920, is an internationally honoured naval architect and his brother Angel, born in 1926, has a doctorate in Spanish-American history, was Director of the Spanish Institute and Cultural Attaché of the Spanish embassy in Mexico (1975-91) and is a senior member of several international orders of merit.

Although typical Spanish aristocrats in appearance, bearing and loyalty to the monarchy, The O'Dogherty and his immediate family exude a prideful sensitivity and possessiveness about their Irish roots. They do not consider their family merely former Irish aristocrats; they see the matter in the present and future tenses – as a matter of history and pedigree. There is no arrogance in their attitude – only conviction.

Don Ramon smiles quietly – with amusement and admiration – when he recounts his grandfather Ramon's hubris in launching a formal legal case in the Dublin courts in 1871 to regain title to and return of the family's estates confiscated by the various English regimes in the two previous centuries. The intrepid Spanish naval officer's attempt is viewed by the present O'Dogherty as quixotic rather than frivolous.

The O'Dogherty, who shares descent with the royal O'Neills, is the forty-fourth direct heir to Niall Fiachra who reigned as King of Ulster five hundred years after the birth of Christ. Scholars of Old Gaelic say that the clan patronymic derives from the word 'dochartach' meaning obstructive. This definition would certainly be appropriate when related to the Anglo-Norman invaders' plans to seize the strategically important peninsula of Inishowen, the ancestral land of The O'Dogherty and to eradicate the family's deeply rooted positions of influence in Irish society, which lasted into the eighteenth century.

Dr Don Ramon O'Dogherty made an emotional, enthusiastically received visit to the Inishowen peninsula in 1990 to coincide with the official courtesy recognition of his title by the Chief Herald of Ireland. At a special clan gathering, attended by over two hundred participants from Europe and America, The O'Dogherty was installed – with the ceremonial rites of his ancestors – at the ancient inaugural stone of the Ó Dochartaighs: wearing the traditional embroidered dark-green robe and cloak and wielding the sword of his ancestor, Caothaoir Ruadh, slain by the English at Doon four hundred years before, Dr Don Ramon O'Dogherty was the focus of a poignant memory for the people of Inishowen – and for the clan itself.

The O'Dogherty castle, still standing on Magazine Street in Derry is now a museum visited by over one thousand people each year. An active O'Dogherty clan association organizes periodic international gatherings in Donegal and publishes its own newsletter for members. Dr Ramon The O'Dogherty keeps in touch with his kinsmen – and with the Standing Council of Irish Chiefs – principally through his naval architect brother as his surrogate; Admiral Pascual O'Dogherty's English, says Ramon, is much more fluent than his own. They both attend the clan gatherings.

Affection and respect for The Ó Dochartaigh's position in history endure strongly in Inishowen. From Ballygorman to Muff, from Raphoe to Rathmullen, people have extremely long memories as well as unsettled emotions regarding the violent removal of their hereditary leaders, the lords of Inishowen, by 'alien force'. Their loyalty to the past, however, does not preclude some quixotic thoughts of their own about a future role for a noble O'Dogherty in the politics of modern Ireland.

Fig. 72.

Burt Castle, Inishowen in 1601.

(State papers, Ireland, CCVIII, pt. 2, Apl.-May 1601, No. 71v.)

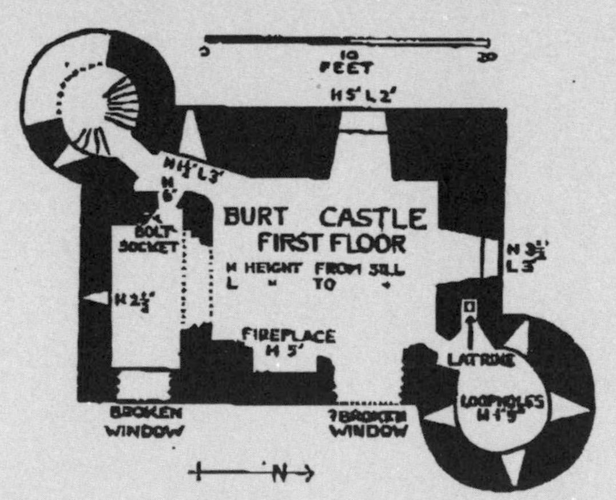


Fig. 73.—Plan of first floor, Burt Castle.

BURT CASTLE, INISHOWEN, CO. DONEGAL

H.G Leask, *Irish Castles* (Dundalk 1951)

# The O'Donnell

## PRINCE OF TIRCONNELL

In virtually every country in the world national legends and sagas are heavily populated with reluctant princes and shy but brave knights: controversy is usually a prime ingredient, mystery adds spice and, almost always, good enduring tales unfold. Ireland is certainly no exception – and The O'Donnell (or O'Donel), Prince of Tirconnell, is the current embodiment of this literary tradition. Hugh O'Donnell (Aodh Ó Dhomhnaill) is very reluctant to discuss his position; his courage is on constant call; and the particulars of the daily challenges that face him are not publicly known; there is also intra-family controversy regarding succession to the title. All the ingredients are at hand.

The O'Donnell – the central figure in this legend-in-progress and principal representative of one of the most historically eminent of the old Gaelic aristocratic families – is a Roman Catholic missionary priest in Africa.

The O'Donnells were kings, chiefs and lords of Tirconnell ('country of the strong wolf') – now Donegal – for over fifteen centuries. Since before the Christian era, as hereditary rulers, they were inaugurated on the sacred Rock of Doon, near Letterkenny. In the fifth century AD, while retaining the inaugural rites of the elder pagan faith, they added the ecclesiastic veneer of a bishop's blessing.

With their territorial neighbours, the powerful O'Neills, kings of Tyrone (and eventually high kings of Ireland) – as allies and periodically as rivals – the O'Donnells controlled the north of Ireland for many generations, prevailing against the attacks and incursions of the English, Normans and Vikings.

Donegal, ancient realm of the princes of Tirconnell is the largest county in Ulster. The O'Donnells' dominance and crucial influence in the province endured until the sixteenth century.

Expanding English military force, along with their settlements, eventually overwhelmed the O'Neill/O'Donnell power. At first they were compelled to exchange their royal Gaelic titles and sovereignties for English earldoms. Although retaining their vast estates, the newly created Earl of Tyrone and Earl of Tirconnell knew that their power had been taken – along with their Gaelic titles and their political independence. After a period of restless peace, the two former Irish princes and their people had a final spasm of insurrection, which failed. In 1607, Tyrone and Tirconnell, with their family, friends and close adherents, fled secretly by ship from Lough Swilly to France. As refugees they travelled, via the royal courts of Europe, to Rome where the royal O'Donnells and O'Neills lived in nostalgic exile until their deaths.

The capitulation and abandonment of their cause was the clear end of an epoque. Judged traitors by English law, The O'Donnell and the O'Neill lands became forfeit. Ulster had been the last stronghold of Gaelic power and tradition; the Tudor conquest was complete, the political and social systems of Gaelic Ireland had been swept away. In the English view, all of Ireland would now lie open for the firm establishment of royal authority under a single crown, bringing a greater degree of stability to the politics of the British Isles.

By the eighteenth century, the Gaelic kingdoms were long gone. The descendants of the noble O'Donnells, however, have held on to the memories of Tirconnell, to the lore and to dynastic respect for the chief of the name. Today, within the House of O'Donnell there are three bits of controversy; Hugh, the incumbent Chief, by his discreet nature, remains virtually silent on the first two matters.

His sister in Dublin – who prefers the traditional spelling – has opted for public comment on an old issue: the succession. Nuala, who has no quarrel with the system of tanistry, nor with her brother's prerogative of selection, has strongly expressed her view, on radio and television, that the female line should not be excluded from succession to the title and that she and her children should be able to claim it.

A point of minor contention, disputed by other members of the family, comes from the descendants of Sir Neil O'Donnell (d. 1821), lst Baronet of Newport House, County Mayo, whose present claimant, a Dubliner, is Aodh (b. 1940), exact contemporary and close cousin of Father Hugh O'Donnell.

A third point of dispute comes quietly from the Spanish branch of the O'Donnells whose claim has been acceptably arguable because of the plethora of O'Donnell branches and the genealogical complication among the descendants of those who fled from Ireland to continental Europe during the Flight of the Wild Geese. Their possible claimant is another namesake, Hugo O'Donnell (b. 1956), a Spanish duke who lives in Madrid.

Presumably, all controversies have now been laid to rest: the Genealogical Office of the Government of Ireland formally confirmed the courtesy recognition of the current chief's position (although Nuala Ní Dhomhnaill persists in her objections to male exclusivity in the succession process); and Father Hugh O'Donnell himself has nominated Hugo, a namesake and a Spanish cousin, as his tanist.

Hugo O'Donnell, 7th Duke of Tetuan, Duke of Estrada, Count of Lucena, Marquis de las Salinas and Marquis of Altamina, descends from the O'Donnells who, as Wild Geese (not Earls), fled annihilation in Ireland and sought refuge – as well as new fortune – in Western Europe. Many of his ancestors became senior military figures: General Hugo The O'Donnell, a Spanish general in the late seventeenth century, served two rival English kings in Ireland, James II and his nemesis, William of Orange; Major General Count O'Donnell, was Minister of Finance for Emperor Franz Josef (and his heirs, the Counts O'Donnell von Tirconnell, are still in Austria); Hugo's ancestors for five generations have been Spanish generals, ministers of finance, war and state, ambassadors and bankers. His great-great-grandfather, Field-Marshal Don Leopoldo (1809-67), became Governor of Cuba – and the paramour of Queen Isabella II of Spain. Hugo himself, a lawyer and amateur historian, served as Minister of Marine under the present king of Spain, Juan Carlos. Hugo – whose large family has pervasive influence in Madrid – will be an effective tanist for the reticent chief of the name. Hugo's father Leopoldo O'Donnell (1915-99), 6th Duke of Tetuan, expressed his family's views to Celtic scholar and author, Peter Berresford Ellis in 1998: 'Perhaps I will not inherit the title of my forebears, nor even my son in his lifetime. But one of my grandsons doubtless will. Our family, forced to flee from our native land to maintain our own existence, has never really abandoned Ireland, our patrimony nor our people of Tirconnell.'

Father Hugh O'Donnell, OFM (Order of Friars Minor, i.e. 'little brothers'), born in Dublin in 1940 and educated there, in Galway and in Rome, was ordained a priest at the age of twenty-five and has been a missionary in Africa for twenty-three years. He is not disdainful of the aristocratic tradition he represents; his reluctance to participate in the obligations relating to his position as Chief of his princely house – or even to discuss the matter – stems from his total dedication to the Franciscan mission and the parish he serves at Riverfall in Harare, Zimbabwe.

With crack-downs on the press, the courts and political opposition, the long-entrenched government of President Mugabe in Zimbabwe has shed any pretence of democratic legitimacy as it struggles for survival. The seizure of white-owned farmland and arrests of journalists amidst growing xenophobia has also posed serious threats to the work of the Franciscan friars. In

2002 Ambassador Thomas McDonald and his deputy, Earl Drury, at the US Embassy in Harare told the author they were fearful for the safety of the clergy.

Exacerbating the civil chaos and political turmoil in Zimbabwe is the devastation of disease: one quarter of the population is infected with AIDS. 160,000 people died in 1999 and 900,000 children were orphaned. Life expectancy in Zimbabwe in 2003 is forty-three years.

It is a touching paradox that Father Hugh O'Donnell, a gentle seeker of peace, is the inheritor of a tradition of tribal turbulence that characterized much of Irish dynastic history for so long – and is also a front-line warrior today against violence and death in south-east Africa. As a man of God, The O'Donnell undoubtedly considers any attention paid to his special lineage an intrusion upon the real point of life and upon his dedication to it. He shuns photographers and interviews.

Father Hugh The O'Donnell is entirely content to leave dynastic issues to his tanist, Don Hugo, who gladly attends the meetings of the Standing Council of Irish Chiefs on his behalf and proudly carries out the duties of the self-exiled scion of the Tirconnell rulers – who remains, by choice, in one of the most dangerous parts of Africa.

DONEGAL CASTLE

From George Wilkinson, *Practical Geology and Ancient Architecture of Ireland,* 1845; Irish Architectural Archive

RANDAL MACDONNELL

# MacDonnell

## OF THE GLENS

In May 1995 the government of Ireland made a determination with regard to the ancient Gaelic family of MacDonnell: Randal MacDonnell of Dublin, listed as an Irish dynast with an Austrian patent of nobility, was officially granted the formal document of courtesy recognition as MacDonnell (Mac Domhnaill) of the Glens, chief of the name, by the Chief Herald Donal Begley. It was reported that meticulous research – and some controversy – had preceded the formal announcement. There had been an unusual dilemma that arose to delay the ultimate approval of the claim. While Randal MacDonnell's roots in Ulster are deep and his lineage unquestionably Gaelic, his main-line male ancestor in the fourteenth century was not Irish; in fact, John MacDonnell (Macdonald) of Argyle, known as Lord of the Isles, was a grandson of Robert II (1315-90), king of Scotland.

In the final analysis, the Chief Herald – assuring himself of the genealogical validity of the claim – had reasoned that the MacDonnell family of the Glens of Antrim had been established in Ireland for almost five hundred years and that their Celtic progenitors had undoubtedly gone to Scotland from Ireland in the first place. Indeed, the Romans had referred to the Irish in Latin as the 'Scotii'. (And, after all, one could add, Antrim is closer to Edinburgh than it is to Dublin.) Recognition granted.

Other dilemmas, however, persist: Randal MacDonnell's application for membership on the Standing Council of Irish Chiefs and his use of the title 'The', are still under consideration. When queried, the incumbent chairman of the Council, The O'Brien, Lord Inchiquin, chose not to elaborate on the points, merely commenting that the matters are on the Council's agenda.

In the thirteenth and fourteenth centuries certain younger sons of the Argyle MacDonnells came to Ireland as mercenary units – gallowglasses – engaged by the most powerful noble chiefs in the north of Ireland. Many of the chiefly family, reigning lords of the isles, returned as a consequence of the marriage of Iain Mhoir MacDonnell to Margery Bisset, the Norman heiress of the Glens in the late fourteenth century. The MacDonnells gradually acquired territory of their own by grants for military service, by other marriages and by outright seizure.

The power of the Irish lords had revived sufficiently to pose a serious problem in military terms for the English government's strategy in Ireland. In the 1300s in particular it proved impossible to maintain effective defenses against the resurgent chieftains in Ulster as well as in the other provinces. With the help of the gallowglasses from Scotland, the Irish leaders – especially in the north – were able to cancel out the military advantages that the Anglo-Norman settlers had enjoyed in the early days of English colonization. England was also being drained by her chronic wars with Scotland and, above all, by the long struggle with France, which was later known by historians as the Hundred Years' War.

As rebel leaders the MacDonnells fought fiercely against the English in both Scotland and Ireland and their victories were triumphantly celebrated. However, after generations of war and rebellion, plus inter and intra-clan conflict – seasoned intermittently with betrayal, murder, hangings, treason and executions – by the middle of the sixteenth century the MacDonnells had been trounced and seduced by, or intermarried with their historic adversaries; they had become faithful subjects of the English sovereign. Sir Randal Arranagh MacSorley MacDonnell soon became Viscount Dunluce and finally was created the 1st earl of Antrim in 1620 by King James I.

With the exception of the 3rd earl – who was tainted by treason for actively espousing the cause of James II in Ireland (but later had his lands and houses restored) – the earls of Antrim had been relatively steady supporters of the Crown and its Anglo-Irish ascendancy. Somhairle Buidhe (anglicized phonetically as 'Sorley Boy') MacDonnell (1505-90), the old patriarch and redoubtable foe of the English, had cast a foreshadow of things to come when he himself finally submitted to the Queen in 1586, forty years before his son Randal accepted an English earldom.

For eight centuries the noble Antrim MacDonnells have been marching through history making strategic marriages and liaisons in a dazzling litany of titles and distinctions: their kith and kin include the Dukes of Norfolk and Buckingham; the Earls of Tyrone, Dungannon, Rutland, Anglesey, Grey, Macclesfield and Shrewsbury; Lords Balfour, Baring, Revelstoke, Milford, Plunkett, Headfort, Londonderry, Lothian and Dunluce; and family connections with the O'Neills, Howards, Villiers, Campbells, Ballochs and Rothermeres.

The extended family of Alexander Randal Mark McDonnell (b. 1935), the current and 9th Earl of Antrim, continues to make its mark: in the House of Lords, as diplomats in the Foreign Office, as Protestant and Catholic clergymen, private secretary to the prime minister, ladies-in-waiting to two queens, senior British army and Royal Navy officers and as prominent publishers, business executives, artists and patrons of the arts.

The seat of the Antrim McDonnells is Glenarm Castle, built in the 1600s near Ballymena, County Antrim, facing the North Channel on the lands of Glenarm that the MacDonnells have possessed for over half a millennium. The oldest core of the noble family was Dunluce Castle, inhabited at least as early as the ninth century, seized from the MacQuillan clan and expanded by the MacDonnells in 1300. The castle was abandoned in 1642 but kept by the family until 1928 when Randal McDonnell, the 7th earl, gave it to the Northern Ireland government for preservation as a national monument. Near the famous golf links of Portrush, the ancient stronghold of Dunluce stands as a vast brooding ruin atop a rocky promontory high above the Atlantic breakers – a stark and dramatic reminder of the MacDonnells' vanished power in Ulster. Here on the ramparts of Dunluce Castle, Sorley Boy mounted cannon salvaged from a wrecked galleon of the Spanish Armada in order to discourage any threats against him as the lord of the Glens or his territory.

Notwithstanding their heraldic and historical prominence, the earls of Antrim have not been eligible, for two hundred years, for recognition (by either the Ulster king-of-arms, Norroy and Ulster or by the chief herald of Ireland) as The MacDonnell, chief of the name, a much older distinction that has its own particular complexities in the matter of succession; nor have the Antrims applied for the recognition. Even the earldom itself developed serious succession complications when a dearth of sons occurred in the eighteenth and nineteenth centuries. This lack of male heirs prompted diversion of the noble and chiefly line in accordance with the strictest interpretation of the rules of primogeniture as well as of the Brehon Law regarding succession.

The 6th earl of Antrim, nevertheless – to preserve the legacy of his own line – obtained a new Royal Patent in 1785 allowing his daughters and their male issue to inherit the earldom by primogeniture. Later, in the early and mid-1800s, the husbands of two Antrim daughters assumed, by Royal Licence, their wives' surname of MacDonnell to further assure the legacy, shiftng the spelling of MacDonnell to McDonnell in the process.

The tradition of Brehon Law, however, as interpreted by the chief herald, ultimately inserted itself in the matter of the more ancient Gaelic title and, in 1995, the chiefly distinction was passed to Randal as the presumed (but not unquestioned) senior direct descendant, in an unbroken male line, of Sorley Boy's great-nephew, Coll Kittagh MacDonnell, who was killed by a kinsman in 1647, but left male heirs. An opposing view, expressed privately by some members of the family, claims that a superior claim to the chieftaincy was waived.

Count Randal MacDonnell (the Christian names 'Randal' and 'Alexander' have been used for centuries by all lines of the family) was born in 1950 in London where his Dublin-born father was chairman of a British television company. A Roman Catholic (like his distant cousin Alexander, the earl of Antrim), Randal often uses the title of Count of the Holy Roman Empire; the title was granted in 1738 – it is claimed – to a collateral ancestor, James MacDonnell, who had fled Ireland with the Wild Geese, joined the service of the Austrian emperor and was given noble rank whose patent allowed it to pass to the male heirs of the first count.

But the complexity of the MacDonnell bloodlines still endures and prompts difficult questions. Hector, uncle of the current earl and distinguished artist and author of *The Wild Geese of the MacDonnells of Antrim*, has nagging doubts about the European titles and says he knows of only two counts in the dynastic family's history: James from County Mayo, count of the Holy Roman Empire in the mid-eighteenth century, who died unmarried and childless; and another MacDonnell from Wicklow who was made a count by the Austrian emperor in the mid-nineteenth century and also died unmarried and with no descendants.

The currently acknowledged MacDonnell, of medium build with a slightly receding line of light brown hair and a chronic restlessness, is amusing and intelligent. He speaks easily on a variety of topics and is voluble about MacDonnell genealogy and Irish history in general. Randal MacDonnell can recite dates and pedigrees with the precision of an ancient Celtic bard. He is not laconic; he can provide a torrent of historical information and claims a strong allergy to anyone who seeks to establish an aristocratic heritage by questionable means. Terence Francis MacCarthy of Belfast and currently of Marrakesh, Morocco, who, a decade ago, marshalled voluminous but, Randal feels, spurious documentation in attempting to be declared The MacCarthy Mór, Prince of Desmond and Lord of Kerslawny, receives Randal's particular ire.

Hector McDonnell, a steadfast devil's advocate in the matter, feels that Randal's ire is a bit ironic. In his judgment, furthermore, it is extremely difficult – if not impossible – to determine who, if any one, is the senior male representative and therefore the rightful The MacDonnell of the Glens. He also considers the identifying phrase 'of the Glens' genealogically untraceable. Hector even wonders if generational data provided to the government's genealogists could have been purposely 'tweaked' and has offered his views to the Office of the Chief Herald.

Randal takes these questions with equanimity, as he displays an official document:

> Office of the Chief Herald
> Heads of Irish Families whose genealogies have been verified
> by the Chief Herald of Ireland
>
> Subject to the possible survival of more senior lines or more senior representatives of the name, at present unidentified, the person named hereunder is recorded at the Genealogical Office as the senior representative of his name and, accordingly is recognized in courtesy with the style MacDonnell of the Glens, Chief of the Name: Count Randal MacDonnell, 94 Fisherman's Wharf, Dublin.
>
> Donal F. Begley
> Chief Herald of Ireland
> Dublin, 16 May 1995

As these matters stir in academic halls and in drawing-rooms, the recognized Chief proceeds with his life. Randal MacDonnell is interested in 'historic architecture'; he created a British television programme based on his book, *Lost Houses*, about historic aristocratic residences in Ireland. He recently established a *pied-à-terre* on Wellington Quay in Temple Bar in Dublin and has acquired a residence in Tangier, Morocco – an odd coincidence in light of his expressed sensitivity to the MacCarthy episode.

Randal MacDonnell is closely involved with the theatre, film and music worlds in Ireland; he has also lived briefly on the upper eastside of Manhattan and spent sixteen years in Los Angeles and Hollywood. He says that he admires actors, writers and musicians and has always thrived in their company. Among other cultural affiliations, MacDonnell is associated with Guinness heir Garech Browne, son of Lord Oranmore and Browne of Castle MacGarrett, Galway, who is the founder of Claddagh Records and patron of the revival of traditional Celtic music in Ireland – notably 'The Chieftains'.

There is an historical coincidence stretching back several centuries to the two unmarried counts MacDonnell: neither Randal, the presumed incumbent chief of the name, nor his brother and tanist, Count Peter MacDonnell, are as yet married. This adds a new twist to the old matter of succession – and to Randal MacDonnell's noble Austrian patent.

With or without further complications, the succession to the noble chieftaincy could eventually provide another paradox: Randal says that, after himself and his brother/tanist Peter, both in their fifties, the nearest eligible male is their seventh cousin, Dr Alastair MacDonnell, also fifty, who lives in

Belfast. Dr MacDonnell, a British subject, was deputy to the former Social Democratic and Labour Party leader, John Hume – and an ardent socialist.

GLENARM CASTLE, CO. ANTRIM
From John Preston Neale, *Views of the Seats of Noblemen and Gentlemen in England, Wales, Scotland and Ireland*, 1818; Irish Architectural Archive

TERENCE MAGUIRE

# The Maguire

## OF FERMANAGH

The Ulster kingdom of Fhear Managh is long gone: the last king died in the sixteenth century. The boundaries of the ancient realm, however, remain roughly the same as those of the present-day county of Fermanagh in Northern Ireland. The watery forested territory comprises 900 square miles – approximately the size of Luxembourg – and stretches south from the cliffs of Magho near Belleek to Newtownbutler. Modern Fermanagh shares borders with County Tyrone and with four counties in the Irish Republic – Donegal, Leitrim, Cavan and Monaghan. Since before the Christian era the hub of this strategically located political entity has been Enniskillen, an energetic, history-laden town standing on an island midway between the upper and lower reaches of the 50-mile-long Lough Erne. Fermanagh is Maguire (MacGuire) country.

The Maguires (Mac or Mág Uidhir, i.e. 'son of Odhar'), as a chiefly presence, were first recorded in AD 957 through the *Annals of Ulster*, a prime source of Irish history. There is historical evidence, tinged with some mythic conjecture, that can trace the lineage of Donn Carrach Maguire, first king of Fermanagh, back to the pre-Christian High King, Cormac Mac Airt (AD 226-266). On firmer genealogical ground, The Maguires are recognized as kings of Fermanagh from 1260 to 1608 with sixteen blood-line Maguire rulers.

The Maguires were known as wise, efficient rulers who filled their courts with poets, historians and learned men of many disciplines. The Maguire kings also became renowned as great benefactors of the Church, recognizing in the thirteenth century that ecclesiastical power would nicely complement their regal power. As both spiritual and temporal rulers they were able to complete their benevolent domination of Fermanagh – and to exercise influence beyond the kingdom. For generations the ruling Maguire dynasty provided archbishops, bishops, archdeacons, abbots and priors to many communities within and outside of their own territory.

Under ever-increasing English pressure, however, the Maguires were forced to yield their sovereignty and had to become 'Princes of Fermanagh'. The final curtain came down on the Maguire kings in 1608 upon the death of Cúchonnacht III, who died (or was murdered) in exile in Genoa where he had continued to plot against the English and to plan for a triumphant return to Fermanagh as the legitimate heir to the last king, Giolla Patrick (1538–40). In the surrender-and-regrant policy of the English, the Maguires had descended in level from king to prince and finally to acceptance of an English baronetcy intended to replace their noble Gaelic legacy.

Cúchonnacht III had not capitulated with grace. He is remembered, by the people of Fermanagh and scholars of the long Anglo-Irish conflict, as the heroic Gaelic nobleman and rebel who purchased a vessel in Rouen, France and returned in it to Lough Swilly for a grim purpose: there, in a final spasm of desperation, Cúchonnacht (in the words of the current Maguire):

> assembled his besieged noble peers – the Great O'Neill, aged, worn out and broken-hearted, the young tempestuous Red Hugh O'Donnell, The MacMahon, The O'Hagan, with twenty-nine cohorts – and, on September 14, 1607, sailed out of Rathmullen carrying the virtual core of Ulster's Gaelic nobility into exile, never to return.

A number of the Maguires, through favours granted by the Crown, retrieved a vestige of their former position as Barons of Enniskillen. The knighthoods and baronetcies were mostly bestowed in the early part of the seventeenth century. Brian Maguire was created Lord Baron of Enniskillen in 1626 by King Charles I and his son Conor succeeded to the title. Of all the barons he was the most famous – or infamous, depending on one's politics or religion: he and Rory O'More were the prime movers in what became known as the 'O'More/Maguire Plot' that led to the 1641 Rebellion and Maguire to the scaffold at Tyburn on 20 February 1645. All of the Maguire barons were Catholic.

The fortunes of the senior branch of the Maguire nobility improved under the Stuart kings: they served as senior officers in James II's army and in the Anglo-Irish Jacobite parliament in Dublin, recouping some land in Fermanagh along with the prospect of increased influence in the future. All possessions and renewed prospects for these former princes of Fermanagh and barons of Enniskillen, however, disappeared in the calamitous defeat of the Jacobite forces at the battles of Aughrim and the Boyne (1690–91). Dozens of the Maguires joined hundreds of their fellow Irish aristocrats in the Flight of the Wild Geese to permanent exile in Europe. Maguire descendants still live in France and Austria where their forebears were so sympathetically accepted at the royal courts.

The incumbent chief of the name, The Maguire of Fermanagh (14th Baron of Enniskillen in the old Stuart dynasty's Jacobite peerage), was born in Belfast. He lives with his wife, the former Patricia Haslam, in Mount Merrion, a pleasant residential section of Dublin. The Chief and Madam Maguire, an amateur painter and bridge player, have two daughters – one a teacher and the other a solicitor – and five grandchildren.

The Maguire is a Catholic whose family line also included many Protestants. Although broad-minded on matters of politics, religion and descent, he subscribes to the Brehon Law regarding succession to ancient Gaelic titles. Uncle of the genealogically discredited Terence MacCarthy, his calm, measured process of reasoning and mediation, combined with his fund of historical knowledge, have earned The Maguire high respect among his peers. Terence Maguire played the leading role in the establishment of the Standing Council of Irish Chiefs on 5 October 1991.

The Maguire, an accountant by training, became a successful businessman and company director, spending much of his professional time in China buying porcelain and *objets d'art*, while developing an extensive personal understanding and affection for the Chinese people. His interest in the Orient remains extremely keen.

Terence Maguire, casual in his dress and manner, is intellectually precise and scholarly. Since retirement from active business affairs in the late 1980s, he has devoted close attention to writing a comprehensive history of the Maguires. The Maguire, in addition, has been intensely dedicated for more than a decade to a unique quest linked to Ireland's history and to his own ancient heritage – 'The Ancient Maguire Chalices'.

During the Bronze Age Irish craftsmen worked in gold and today such items as gold torcs and lunulae, showing great skill and craftsmanship, can be seen in Irish museums. With the coming of Christianity, Ireland entered an era of extraordinary craftsmanship, exemplified, by the Tara brooch and the magnificent Ardagh chalice. During the Viking raids, periodic invasions and the suppression of the monasteries, many of such treasures disappeared. During the period from the end of the fifteenth century to the mid-eighteenth century the Irish nobility steadily declined along with their patronage of the arts. The Maguires, however, continued patronage through four centuries with their chalices of 1493, 1529, 1633, 1739 and 1751. These icons are unique in that they mirror, not only the fortunes of the Maguires, but also the changing face of Ireland in each succeeding century.

Following the Reformation and the defeat of the Gaelic order in the first part of the seventeenth century, only a small number of these early chalices have survived: one is now in Scotland and the other was in England. Later, during a period of relative peace and accommodation between the newly planted English and the old Irish aristocrats, the immediate descendants of the deposed Maguire kings revived their family's tradition of patronage: from the mid-1600s to the mid-1700s, they again commissioned a number of the beautiful chalices to present to their religious centres. Two of the precious artefacts of the later period survive – both in the Republic of Ireland.

At his own expense The Maguire devoted thousands of hours of research, historical detective work, correspondence and international travel in pursuit of his dream – to locate, repatriate and put on permanent display the extraordinary 'Maguire chalices' created centuries ago by a fusion of spiritual zeal and stunning Irish craftsmanship. With unprecedented co-operation from both Catholic and Protestant churches, government officials, art connoisseurs and private individuals, The Maguire has found the four surviving treasures: The Great Medieval Maguire Chalice of 1493, for centuries possessed and guarded by the ancient clan of Mac Leod at Dunvegan Castle on the Isle of Skye in Scotland; The King Cúchonnacht Maguire I Chalice of 1529, at St Mary's Church in Fernyhalgh, Lancaster, England; the Princess Maire Maguire (daughter of King Cúchonnacht Maguire III) Chalice of 1633, held by the Redemptionist Church in Quebec; and the Sir Bryan Maguire Crested 'Penal' Chalice of 1751 at St Clare's Church at Manorhamilton, County Leitrim.

The Maguire – who was faced with serious health problems in 2003 – considers his search a contribution towards a more sophisticated perspective of his country:

> I hope I can carry on. I have been privileged, as chief of the name, to engage in my quest. The Maguire chalices have become an integral part of my life and I have become very much aware of the ever-deepening interest – in the north and south of this divided island – in the history of Irish life and culture. The chalices provide important evidence of the spirituality and artistic skills of our ancestors.

Terence Maguire, whose tanist has not yet been identified, has a patrician nose, a broad forehead and a courtly air. This chief of the name sees his noble ilk as representing a needed link to Ireland's past – and to its vibrant present.

ENNISKILLEN CASTLE WATERGATE, 'PENAL' CHALICE,
GREAT MEDIEVAL CHALICE (ENGRAVING),
GREAT MEDIEVAL CHALICE

MUNSTER

CONOR MYLES JOHN O'BRIEN

# The O'Brien

## PRINCE OF THOMOND

Since 1984 guests at the imposing Dromoland Castle in County Clare on the west coast of Ireland have often been pleasantly surprised to be invited to an hour's lecture on the history of the famous baronial estate and of the illustrious family whose seat it was for centuries. The talks – followed by questions from a captive audience – take place about eight times a year in the elegant East Drawing Room of the castle formerly known as the Music Room; during the autumn and winter months there is usually a crackling log-fire in the grate behind the speaker and in the spring and summer the wide, high windows and French doors open to the winding paths leading to the lakes, woods and fields that comprise the ancient Dromoland demesne.

The lecturer is most often Conor Myles John The O'Brien, Prince of Thomond, the 18th Baron Inchiquin (Lord Inchiquin), 10th Baronet of Leamaneagh – and the 32nd direct male descendent of Brian Boru, supreme monarch or ard rí of Ireland who died a millennium ago. Conor O'Brien is chief of the name and one of the three claimants to the high kingship of Ireland.

The walls of the main salons, dining and reception rooms and the principal hallways of Dromoland Castle are hung with large oil portraits of noble O'Briens and their spouses – commissioned, purchased, or presented to the family over many generations. A large (17' x 10') painting – done in the seventeenth century – of Brian Boru's grandson, King Donough I, sword held aloft and astride his rearing stallion, with Limerick Cathedral in the background, now hangs in the corridor adjacent to the former study of past resident chiefs, which was transformed into a cocktail bar when the venerable Dromoland Castle passed into American hands in 1962 after nineteen generations of possession by the royal House of O'Brien.

❧

The O'Briens, princes of Thomond (north Munster) as well as barons Inchiquin, one of the few native Irish noble houses now in the British peerage, descend in an unbroken line from Brian Boru who became king of the kings in Ireland in 1002 and was slain in battle on Good Friday, 23 April 1014 at the decisive victory of the Irish over the Danes at Clontarf on the east coast north of Dublin. Every schoolchild in modern Ireland should know that date.

The real but legendary ard rí, from whom the family takes its name, was succeeded by a long line of monarchs and princes – high kings as well as provincial rulers in subsequent generations – which came to an end as a reigning dynasty at the death of the current chief's direct ancestor, Murrough O'Brien, King of Thomond who died in 1578, sixteenth in descent from Brian Boru. During Murrough's reign, the O'Briens submitted to Henry VIII of England who in lieu granted them the earldom of Thomond and the barony of Inchiquin.

In the annals of Irish history the royal O'Brien lines carry back long before their patronymic ancestor, Brian, who, through shrewd state-craft, military prowess and extraordinary vigour, had unified the fractious noble houses of Ireland under one monarchy. The O'Briens are descendants of Milesius, King of Spain, through his sons Heber, Heremon and Ir, who reputedly led the Milesian invasion of south-west Ireland and supposedly settled there about the time of Alexander the Great in the fourth century before Christ. The Milesians established the dynasties of the ruling Gaelic families, including the O'Briens, the O'Neills and the O'Conors.

In a genealogical debate regarding the high kingship, the O'Brien claim may be hypothetically paramount over the O'Conor and O'Neill claims since the O'Briens are descended most directly from Heber, the third son of King Milesius, while the O'Conor and the O'Neills are from the junior branches of Heremon, the eighth son. Mythic or historic, these ancestors from Galicia have real meaning to genealogists and historians in Ireland; there are only thirty-two generations between Conor O'Brien, the current claimant and Brian Boru; and only 120 generations since the sire of them all came from Spain.

Memories are long in Ireland – so are the records of the Irish aristocrats. The pedigree of the Dromoland O'Briens, held in a vault at Lloyds in London, stretches more than thirty-six feet.

As the high kingship established by Brian Boru declined and finally splintered into the old historic provincial realms, the royal O'Briens of Thomond survived as regional over-lords for centuries by adapting – at first reluctantly, then gradually and later successfully – to the spreading power of the Anglo-Normans. (In some areas the noble hereditary oligarchies lasted into the seventeenth century – and some families held their sway, in one form or another, even into the twentieth century.)

After the Reformation, a major factor in the conflict between the old Gaelic order and the expanding 'foreign' ascendancy was, of course, religion. Strong Catholics and aggressive defenders of the faith since the earliest days of Christianity, the noble O'Briens' church allegiance in the later centuries, like those of most of the old aristocratic Catholic families, very often fluctuated with the prevailing power structures; submission, marriage, military alliance and other devices of accommodation were involved in changing a family's spiritual affiliation from Roman Catholic to 'Established Church', i.e. Anglican Protestant, and sometimes vice versa.

In those uncertain times it was not rare for an aristocratic family to play the odds by splitting their ecclesiastic vote: one member would be chosen to convert (usually termed 'conform') in order for the family to have influence on both sides if the need arose. This religious-political see-saw is well chronicled in The O'Brien's family history. The present Chief is a Protestant.

A faint echo of this traditionally mercurial relationship between religion and politics in Ireland was heard in 1937 when Éamon de Valera, icon of Irish independence and soon-to-be-president of a newly born Republic of Ireland, reputedly approached in private Donough The O'Brien of Thomond, the 16th Lord Inchiquin – and uncle of the current claimant – with a proposal that was daring by modern standards, but historically familiar in Ireland: de Valera, obsessed by the vocation to preserve or re-establish the ancient Gaelic traditions, suggested that The O'Brien, a member of the Church of Ireland, become, by mandate or referendum, the Prince-President of Ireland. De Valera and not a few others, saw this as a rightful return of the old native ruling house that would then reign ultimately over a 'United Ireland' – a phrase that has become a fierce rallying cry for today's mainly Catholic Irish nationalists and anathema for the Protestant (predominantly Presbyterian) loyalists in Northern Ireland who want to remain subjects of Her Britannic Majesty.

Journalists speculated, at the time of President de Valera's rumoured proposition, about which part of the Chief's heritage would prevail in his decision – the royal O'Brien or the baronial Inchiquin. Presumably after discussion with his wife, the Honourable Anne Thesiger, daughter of Lord Chelmsford, a former viceroy of India and their two daughters, Deirdre and Grania, The O'Brien decided, for personal reasons, to reject the possibility of occupying the long empty throne of Ireland and to remain a private anglicized Irish citizen in the space and comfort of his Dromoland estates.

(President de Valera's unabashed support for aristocratic traditionalism and for Gaelic hegemony were very similar to the deep-seated royalist and Gallic sympathies of his fellow chief-of-state, General Charles de Gaulle. During World War II, as leader of the Free French and later as President of France, de Gaulle had secretly discussed with Winston Churchill and with confidants his private hope that the House of Bourbon-Orléans, in the person of the claimant, His Royal Highness, Monseigneur Henri d' Orléans, the Count of Paris, could be restored to the throne of France in a post-war constitutional monarchy. De Gaulle's vision was not rebuffed by the enthusiastic French claimant, as de Valera's had been by Donough O'Brien/Inchiquin; de Gaulle's secret aspiration was simply overwhelmed by cascading political events in Europe.)

For reasons of health and financial concerns, in the early 1960s Donough The O'Brien, sixteenth Baron of Inchiquin, decided to sell Dromoland Castle – along with a parcel of 400 acres of land plus shooting and fishing rights – to an American businessman, Bernard McDonough from West Virginia, whose grandparents had lived not far from Newmarket-on-Fergus, the village closest to the estate. McDonough converted the castle into a deluxe resort hotel in 1963.

Following the sale of the castle, Donough and Madam O'Brien still retained a thousand acres of the Dromoland demesne; they built a handsome Georgian residence, Thomond House, for themselves and their successors on a hill less than a quarter of a mile from their previous home.

Upon Donough O'Brien's death in 1968 at the age of seventy-one, the title and claim to the ancient throne passed to his next younger brother, Phaedrig O'Brien, as the 17th Baron and chief of the name. Phaedrig – a former British army major, coffee planter and mining executive in East Africa – and his English wife, Vera Winter, lived at Thomond House and managed the Dromoland estates farming operations until he died, childless, in May 1982. Phaedrig's nephew, Conor Myles John O'Brien succeeded him as The O'Brien, Prince of Thomond and 18th Baron of Inchiquin, chief of the name and claimant. Conor, then a bachelor, moved to Thomond House in 1983.

After the death of Bernard McDonough, following a long illness the previous year, Dromoland Castle, by then a well-functioning hotel, was purchased from his widow in 1987 by a small group of American, Irish and Spanish investors. In the intervening years three major stages of expansion and renovation have transformed the ancient property into a proud and successful reflection of its turbulent past.

The first O'Brien castle at Dromoland had been built as a defensive stronghold in the fifteenth century during their tenure as high kings –

although the family had owned the land for four centuries before that. The second Dromoland Castle, built in 1736, was more residential in the softer Queen Anne style. The present main building of the castle, in the Gothic style, was completed in 1826 after fifteen years of construction. The next dramatic changes, after McDonough's initial conversion in 1963, was accomplished by the American-led syndicate in the 1980s and 1990s when Dromoland Castle emerged as a world-class, historically significant hotel and sporting destination.

❧

Conor Myles John The O'Brien is an excellent lecturer: he knows his subjects thoroughly and has the skill of conveying information and knowledge interestingly – embellished by an engaging sense of humour and a finely tuned historical perspective. Being a living relic of the subject he is lecturing about gives him a special cachet with audiences. Conor O'Brien articulates his material clearly with a deep voice and in the crisp accent learned during his childhood and schooling in England.

Several years ago a lady guest at Dromoland Castle, a Canadian archaeologist, described Conor O'Brien, rather cryptically, as 'having an Etruscan profile'; although unmistakably English or Irish in his ways and manner of speaking, he has the lean, dark look of a southern European, possibly French – or (shades of Milesius?) Spanish.

When The O'Brien is unable to give the lectures at Dromoland Castle, his first cousin, the Honourable Grania O'Brien Weir, daughter of Conor's late uncle Donough, Lord Inchiquin, is a popular replacement. Married to fellow author, scholar and publisher Hugh Weir and living in Whitegate, County Clare, nearby in O'Brien territory, Grania Weir was private secretary to the British ambassadors in Peru and Japan, to two members of Parliament and social secretary to Mrs John Hay Whitney, wife of the US ambassador to the Court of St James's during the Eisenhower administration. Grania Weir, who grew up at Dromoland Castle, is an accomplished lecturer and a recognized authority on the royal O'Briens.

Conor The O'Brien was born in Surrey, England, on 17 July 1943, the son of the youngest son of the 15th Baron Inchiquin. He has one sister, Fiona O'Brien Obert de Thieusies, who lives in Belgium and in London. Conor was educated at Eton, served as an officer in the British Army in the Middle East, Far East and in Europe from 1962 to 1975 and has worked most of his life abroad. After almost a decade in Hong Kong and Singapore as a trading company executive and banker, he returned to live in Ireland in 1982 when he succeeded his uncle Phaedrig.

In 1988 The O'Brien married Helen Farrell of Newtown Forbes, County Longford, in Quin Parish Church a few miles from Dromoland. They have two lively and charming daughters, the Honourable Slaney O'Brien (b. 1989) and the Honourable Lucia O'Brien (b. 1991) who, after a few years in the local Catholic school in Newmarket-on-Fergus, went to a private school in Dublin. Conor O'Brien's tanist or heir apparent has not yet been identified. The and Madam O'Brien, a friendly, striking brunette, take recommended paying guests at Thomond House and have turned the Dromoland estates into a major sporting centre, which is co-ordinated with the Dromoland Castle hotel activities: driven pheasant shooting, deer stalking, fishing, horse-riding, falconry, eventing, hunter trials and archery. The O'Brien is also chairman of two land development companies and has served as chairman of the Standing Council of Irish Chiefs.

Conor O'Brien organized the worldwide O'Brien Clan Association and, in 1992, held the first clan gathering for four hundred years; in 2003 there was a festival in Killaloe, County Clare, commemorating the one thousandth anniversary of the accession of Brian Boru to the high kingship of Ireland.

Helen O'Brien shares the duties and responsibilities that are an integral part of their special position. At last count in 2002, they gave eighty-six speeches – Conor forty-nine and Helen thirty-seven – most of them to foreign and Irish tourists who come in groups to Thomond House for the well-known programme of cocktails and dinner followed by a lecture on the Dromoland O'Briens: being a royal pretender and keeper-of-the-flame can be hard work. The O'Brien, a-not-so-hidden-aristocrat and Irish Chief, views his position as business – a labour intensive business.

If so, it is also a remarkably durable family enterprise with an unchanging business address. The royal O'Briens have been running Dromoland for over one thousand years.

DROMOLAND CASTLE ENTRANCE, CO. CLARE
Courtesy Patrick Rossmore; Irish Architectural Archive

DON JUAN O'CALLAGHAN

# The O'Callaghan

## LORD OF CLONMEEN

The O'Callaghan, one of the nine hereditary chiefs of the name who live outside Ireland, has been a resident of Barcelona most of his life; his branch of this ancient aristocratic family arrived in Spain over three hundred years ago. Conchobar (Conor) O'Callaghan, ancestor of the current Chief fled from Ireland in the late 1600s as a refugee from the events that had devastated his family's position and threatened the lives of the clan's leaders.

O'Callaghans – in various ways – had been escaping death and ruin in their own land for many generations. As Irish nobles and military officers, many were well received in the royal courts of England's enemies in Europe: Conchobar O'Callaghan became a captain in the Irish Brigade of the Spanish army, while his brother Sean was a captain in O'Brien's regiment of the Irish Brigade in the French army and was later created a baron by the grateful king of France. Historical records of the O'Callaghans in Spain are extensive in the Spanish royal archives and public libraries.

The present head of the clan is Don Juan O'Callaghan, The O'Callaghan, Lord of Clonmeen, whose noble house descends directly in the male line from Ceallachaín Chaisel (Callaghan of Cashel), king of Munster in the tenth century and eponymous ancestor of the sept or clan. Ceallachaín's predecessors had been hereditary rulers since the early Christian era in Ireland. Similar to the other royal, princely and chiefly houses, the O'Callaghans endured as political and social factors in Ireland until the sixteenth century.

For half a millennium, as the military expeditions – which had been sent to Ireland from England by Henry II in the twelfth century – turned gradually from invasion to conquest, the resilient O'Callaghans were dispossessed several times. Like many of their fellow provincial rulers they lost their power and their properties after the Anglo-Norman invasion, during Oliver Cromwell's regime three hundred years later and finally during the confiscations that followed Catholic King James II's defeat by his Protestant son-in-law and successor, William of Orange.

During the politically complex but relatively stable eras between major military defeats, some of the O'Callaghans took advantage of the surrender-and-regrant policy to keep possession of their land and, in the bargain, to preserve their patents of nobility for political purposes. Some married into the increasingly powerful Anglo-Norman Protestant families, producing the precursors of the special breed known as the Anglo-Irish. Others, among the O'Callaghan clan's leading families, fled for their lives.

Don Juan O'Callaghan's ancestor came to Spain to escape the Penal Laws These restrictions, prompted by an iron-fisted political policy of crushing all vestiges of the former Gaelic system, bore most heavily upon the Irish gentry; the Penal Code was basically directed against them. The peasantry were not regarded as dangerous at that time, but the few surviving Roman Catholic aristocratic proprietors were – and Conchobar O'Callaghan was one of them.

Land was the key to political power and the Parliament was determined that it should not pass into or return to Roman Catholic hands. The Penal Laws, created solely to ensure this policy, were extraordinarily draconian: Roman Catholics were forbidden to acquire land from a Protestant by purchase, inheritance, or gift, nor could they lease it for a longer time than thirty-one years. A Roman Catholic proprietor had no power to leave land by will. On his death it was to be divided among his sons. But if the eldest became a Protestant he was to inherit it all; if his conversion took place during his father's lifetime, the father became merely a life-tenant, without power to divide part of the estate. If a Protestant woman, owning land, married a Roman Catholic her land passed at once to the Protestant next of kin; if a Roman Catholic wife turned Protestant all her property was released from her husband's control.

These were the Penal Law provisions relating only to the matter of land. Those dealing with education, religion, marriages, the professions, agriculture, fishing, commerce, dress and virtually all aspects of ordinary life were similarly severe.

Over the centuries the O'Callaghans clan's ruling families had been disenfranchized and forced to abandon their ancestral lands several times – by their neighbouring Irish adversaries as well as by the Anglo-Normans. In the twelfth century they were forcibly shifted by the O'Briens from what is the present County Clare in Connacht to the barony of Clonmeen, near Mallow in north Cork where the clan has been entrenched for centuries. During the Cromwellian confiscations the leading family of the clan was forcibly transplanted back to Clare. The humbler members of the clan, in accordance with the occupiers' policy, were not uprooted; they remained in Cork where most O'Callaghans have been concentrated ever since.

The hereditary ruling contingent that had been moved to Clare was led by the incumbent O'Callaghan chief whose descendants today include the family of O'Callaghan-Westropp of Lismehane near the village of O'Callaghan's Mills in east Clare.

While several dozen of the O'Callaghan aristocrats had escaped to Europe, the immediate family of the chief of the name continued to live in Ireland – with its seat at Kilgorey in County Clare. When Eamonn (Edmond) The O'Callaghan was killed in a duel at a horse-fair in south Clare at the end of the eighteenth century, leaving only daughters, the title was passed (by consensus without formal derbhfine authority) to the Spanish cousin, Don Ramon O'Callaghan (1765-1833), the descendant of Conchobar. The Clare branch, as represented by the O'Callaghan-Westropp family, and the Spanish branch disputed the title of The O'Callaghan for 185 years – until, in 1976, the Genealogical Office of the Irish government finally and officially gave courtesy recognition of the title to Don Juan O'Call-aghan (1903-79), a prominent solicitor based in Tortosa, Spain. His son, Don Juan O'Callaghan Casas, born in 1934, inherited the title.

The current head of the ancient princely house is a private, scholarly man with a dry sense of humour, steady brown eyes and a hawk-like nose. An independent consulting engineer, The O'Callaghan received a doctorate in electrical engineering from the University of Barcelona. The Chief's second son, another Don Juan, born in 1963, has been named as tanist. The younger O'Callaghan, also a prominent engineer, holds doctorates from the University of Barcelona where he is a professor and from the University of Wisconsin. Both father and son live active professional lives and are highly respected intellectually and socially in their Barcelona communities.

Don Juan O'Callaghan is very proud of his Catalan background and of his antecedents' distinguished records in Spanish history. He is also keenly aware of his position as The O'Callaghan, chief of the name, dynastic head of his princely house. As a member of the Standing Council of Irish Chiefs, he visits Ireland at least once a year and corresponds regularly with members of his clan.

Don Juan is stirred with emotion, he says, when he ponders the traceable direct line back to his ancestor Ceallachaín, the forty-second king of Munster who died over a thousand years ago. It is also provocative for scholars of Celtic pre-Christian history to consider that the progenitors of most of the principal royal houses of Ireland were the sons of Milesius, the king of Spain. In the final historical analysis, perhaps the Milesian O'Callaghans simply 'came home'.

DROMANEEN CASTLE, CO. CORK
Office of Public Works

FREDERICK JAMES O'CARROLL

# The O'Carroll

## PRINCE OF ELY

Sociologists and political analysts seem to agree that there are approximately forty million Americans 'of Irish extraction' – almost 15 per cent of the US population and eight times the combined populations of the Irish Republic and Northern Ireland. Of the twenty current heads of the princely Irish dynasties who have been officially granted courtesy recognition by the Government of Ireland, only one lives in the USA. (There are none in Canada or in Latin America.)

Frederick James, The O'Carroll of Ely (Ó Cearbhall Éile), chief of the name, lives quietly in central California where he was born in 1933,but peace and tranquillity surely did not characterize the history of the O'Carrolls in Ireland over the past centuries; both family and public records bristle with violence, intrigue and dramatic changes in fortune. While Fred O'Carroll knows well the vivid saga of his Gaelic ancestors, he cherishes equally his immediate family's role in the settlement and expansion of the American West, which had its own brand of turbulence.

The noble O'Carrolls descend directly from Cearbhall (Carroll), King of Éile (Ely), a territory in the modern counties of Tipperary and Offaly in the provinces of Munster and Leinster the centre of which encompassed the towns of Birr, Roscrea and Nenagh. King Cearbhall, an ally of King Brian Boru, was killed with him in battle at the decisive Irish victory over the Danes at Clontarf in 1014.

The Old Kingdom of Éile (or Ely), comprising 160 square miles, was subordinate to the monarchs of Munster, the royal ancestors of Cearbhall. It served as a bastion of Gaelic dynastic strength against the spreading invaders: the O'Carrolls were well-organized and militarily sophisticated. The Kingdom of Ely for several centuries was a buffer zone that successfully impeded the encroaching Anglo-Norman power – until its ruler, King

Domhnall Fionn Cearbhall, was brutally slain by the Normans in the early part of the thirteenth century. The O'Carrolls turned provisionally to a subtler war-time tactic: the strategic marriage.

Several of the dynastic O'Carrolls, for reasons of security, married into the families of the great Anglo-Norman lords – such as the Butlers who had become the Dukes of Ormond. Before the advent of the Norman Butlers, the O'Carrolls possessed very extensive territory in Tipperary – and, even earlier, had ruled in Leix and Kilkenny – but were later restricted by English authority to the district around Birr in Offaly. Birr Castle, now a tourist attraction, was the medieval stronghold of the O'Carrolls and seat of the senior branch until internal disputes eventually undermined the strength of the rulers of Ely. Leap Castle, another fifteenth century seat south-east of Birr, which fortified the valley between Leinster and Munster, had a sinister reputation as one of the most haunted castles in Europe – particularly because of an unusually 'smelly ghost' described by both William Butler Yeats and Oliver St John Gogarty. Burnt down in 1922, the ruins of Leap Castle still stand as a reminder of the vanished power of the Elyans.

At the death of their king, Donnchadh Cearbhall in the mid-fourteenth century, the family dropped the regal title; The O'Carroll henceforth used the title of 'Prince of Ely'. The formal submission of the chief of the name to the English Crown in 1537 had caused the political fortunes of the princely O'Carrolls to move in different directions.

During the previous century several of the influential O'Carroll noblewomen had married into the other princely Gaelic families – including the powerful O'Donnells and O'Neills – thereby creating a situation where the O'Carrolls were, in effect, divided into two factions: one that had married strategically, relinquished their Gaelic title and sovereignty and paid feudal tribute to the English kings in return for a baronetcy protected by the invaders' law of primogeniture; and the other faction, fiercely loyal to their Gaelic traditions and constant in their hatred of the English, which employed the power of the derbhfine and the force of the ancient Brehon Law – reinforced by the long swords of the O'Carroll sept – to purge their English-seduced clansmen from its leadership and to retain their ancestral lands.

During the sixteenth century the disputes within the extended noble family itself, as well as their struggles against the English Crown, pitted brother against brother in the claims to the title of The O'Carroll, Prince of Ely. Assassinations, blood feuds and enduring intrigue plagued the O'Carrolls for generations. In spite of the unremitting tightening of the Anglo-Norman – or, more generally, English – supremacy, The O'Carrolls had been able to keep vast property in their ancestral area; their sept retained its Gaelic way of life and much of its independence until the end of the 1600s.

But the disintegration had started. As Celtic historian and author Peter Berresford Ellis wrote in 1998, 'The concept of the old Kingdom of Ely was almost completely gone. The O'Carrolls were soon to become merely anglicized knights with large land-holdings.' Still, the process of conquest (an early version of the modern 'ethnic cleansing') was not able to easily abolish the forceful, tenacious Brehon rules of succession that insured the old Gaelic princely lines would carry on.

Many of the O'Carrolls rose to defend the reigning Catholic Stuart dynasty in England against its domestic and foreign enemies and distinguished themselves as loyal Jacobites in the armies of King James II and of France. During the relatively peaceful period for the old (but increasingly anglicized) Irish aristocrats, before the collapse of the Jacobite dream at James II's defeat, The O'Carroll of that era had shifted his centre of interest to Dublin where he became Lord Mayor and a full supporter of his Catholic Majesty's reign in Ireland. Peace and prosperity for the 'old blood' was short lived, however.

When the Jacobite forces were eventually crushed, the mostly Protestant conquerors swept in for possession; in the fury of victory the troops of Prince William of Orange, slew almost to a man all the O'Carroll opposition that had been led by its last, near-mythic hero, Antoine Fada (Long Anthony), The O'Carroll of Emmell Castle. Long Anthony had previously led a slaughter of Dutch Williamites in a bog near the Barna Gap. His later defeat was the final spasm of the ancient O'Carroll dynasty's fight for Gaelic survival against the alien forces. Many had died, most were dispossessed and hundreds of the senior branches of the noble O'Carrolls fled to Europe as Wild Geese.

In the early 1700s, half a century after the Williamite victory, Long Anthony's great-grandson, Richard, lost all the remaining O'Carroll lands and other assets in Ireland. According to bitter family lore, Richard O'Carroll was a feckless, spendthrift addicted to gambling and ambitious ladies.

A cousin of the profligate Richard – Charles Carroll (1737-1815) whose grandfather had emigrated to the American colonies – became a signatory of the Declaration of Independence, a congressman and senator, an influential Catholic layman, the founder of Carrollton, Maryland and reputedly the richest man in the United States.

A hundred years later, James O'Carroll, another kinsman and great-grandfather of the current chief of the name, came, at the age of eleven in 1851, with his parents to New York where his son, Michael Frederick O'Carroll (1864-1938), the present O'Carroll's grandfather, was born.

Frederick James O'Carroll, the incumbent Prince of Ely, is a western American to the core. He is proud of his ancestors' courage and strength in making the often perilous and sometimes disastrous trek westward to the new US frontier. Originally from Redding in northern California and educated at Modesto and Ambassador, two small local colleges, The O'Carroll lives in Ceres, a city of 32,000, close to Modesto, set in the northern San Joaquin Valley, about sixty miles east of San Francisco. His maternal great-grandfather, George Bertram Lander, was born on a wagon train in the 1860s en route from Fort Wayne, Indiana, to Salem, Oregon. The Landers, cattle ranchers by tradition, later settled in the Mount Shasta/Red Bluff/Redding areas of California. Fred O'Carroll's great-grandmother (Katherine Isham Lander) was Abraham Lincoln's niece.

In the late 1800s The O'Carroll's paternal grandfather, Mike O'Carroll, went from New York to Texas where he was a railroad contractor in charge of construction on the Nevada-California rail line, pushing its way through to Oregon to form the NC&O Railroad. Fred O'Carroll – who is called 'Ely' by many of his family and friends – recounts with delight his grandfather's tales of gun battles and outlaws that punctuated the railroad's expansion to the northwest. The railroader's son, Winfrey Frederick (1909-69), The O'Carroll's father, moved from Oregon to California in the 1930s.

The O'Carroll was an enlisted man in the US Navy for twelve years – in Korea, 1953-62 and during the Vietnam war, 1966–70 – serving in the Intelligence and Communications sections. Before his retirement from business in 1987, Fred had been associated with a trucking company and a tank trailer manufacturing operation near Redding with his brother and his son. Since then, the chief of the name has also operated an organization to foster O'Carroll clan activities and tourist visits to the former royal O'Carroll realm in Ireland.

The O'Carroll and his first wife, Agnes Hiemstra, have a son, Frederick Arthur James O'Carroll, who has been named tanist. (By a quirk of historical coincidence, the previous Madam O'Carroll is a descendent of the Anglo-Norman Butlers, the Dukes of Ormond, distant kith of the O'Carroll's.) The present wife of the Hereditary Chief is the former Gracy Ann Block.

Frederick O'Carroll gives the impression of coming directly from a supporting role in a Hollywood western. Of medium height and portly, he has a sandy moustache that droops to join his grey side-burns giving him the grizzled look of a veteran frontier sheriff. Beneath his receding hairline and sun-bronzed forehead, Fred's semi-hooded eyes have a steady, steely gaze. But a smile twitches irrepressively in the corners of his mouth: F.J. O'Carroll is a showman.

The O'Carroll has artfully interwoven his historic Gaelic dimension with his basic American background. Several times a year Fred O'Carroll participates at Gaelic-oriented events in the Pacific NorthWest. He attends as a

Prince-High Chief or as a VIP guest. He has become a familiar personage at the annual two-day Scottish Highland Games in Enumclaw, Washington and at many other clan events. In the Autumn 2000 issue of *Marie Claire*, a nine-page fashion spread featured The O'Carroll at the Highland Games, dancing with tartan-clad models from Tommy Hilfiger, Givenchy, Jimmy Choo and Hermes. In a be-medalled formal military jacket, black tie and pleated white shirt, an O'Carroll tartan kilt fronted by a lynx head sporran and wearing a tam-o-shanter with four hawk feathers, the only Gaelic chief of the name in the western hemisphere was described as being 'totally in his element'.

Aside from a shared heritage and definite genetic links, Frederick James The O'Carroll, Prince of Ely, has no resemblance to and little affinity for the other nineteen chiefs of the name. Although he attends the meetings of the Standing Council of Irish Chiefs and is on good terms with his peers, Fred is different. He is one of only two of the twenty recognized chiefs of the Council to endorse primogeniture over the Brehon system of succession; his dress, accent, perspective and attitude are also unique among his princely colleagues. The O'Carroll, however, concurs with the majority in his unequivocal belief in the importance of re-establishing the ancient Gaelic aristocratic influence in Ireland.

Oddly (and perhaps even disturbingly for the clan), there are still occasional echoes of the violent disputes over The O'Carroll succession; the contentions reach back four centuries to the era when the derbhfine savagely objected to the Tudor-sponsored The O'Carroll, Sir William, and contrived his assassination. In 1915 William O'Carroll of Arabeg, Birr – a direct descendant – had assembled sufficient genealogical documentation to be regarded as the 'senior representative', i.e. The O'Carroll. All particulars of this claim, along with the current holder's genealogical credentials, were scrupulously vetted by experts and courtesy recognition of the title was finally conferred on Frederick James O'Carroll by Office of the Chief Herald of Ireland in 1993. The Arabeg O'Carrolls are silent – but still around.

Genealogists admit that surprises sometimes lurk in the high grass and thickets of dynastic research. Although concerned by serious health problems since 2003, Fred O'Carroll, the quintessentially American possessor of an ancient Irish title of nobility, seems blithely unconcerned about such lingering disputes as he continues to foster the heritage of The O'Carroll as well as the memories of the vanished kingdom of Ely. It gives this would-be king, this chief of the name, particular satisfaction to see today – on several principal motor routes leading into and out of counties Tipperary and Offaly – permanent road signs that say: 'Entering (or Leaving) Ely O'Carroll Country.'

O'CARROLL'S CASTLE, EMMELL WEST, CO. OFFALY
Office of Public Works

DANIEL O'DONOVAN AND HIS WIFE
FRANCES JANE O'DONOVAN

# The O'Donovan

Underneath Daniel O'Donovan's affable, unpretentious manner and his individual style lies a serious pride of position. Morgan Gerald Daniel The O'Donovan (b. 1931), chief of the name, embodies the combination of influences that have produced this long-enduring Gaelic royal line that survives today in modern Ireland.

O'Donovans have been rooted in County Cork for nearly eight hundred years. The current chief of the name and Madam O'Donovan, the former Frances Jane Templer, live at Hollybrook House, a family seat still in the ancestral lands of the clan a few miles north of the town of Skibbereen on the south-western coast of Munster between the Celtic Sea and the Atlantic Ocean. The family's long linkage with that area of West Cork known as Carbery, began after they were expelled from County Limerick – the O'Donovan place of origin – not long after the Norman invasion of Ireland in the early 1200s.

The O'Donovans, hounded by the invaders and slowly forced south also by their Gaelic adversaries, the royal O'Briens of Thomond, accepted mutual protection from the powerful MacCarthy kings so deeply established in western Cork. The O'Donovans have been there ever since.

While the genealogies of the twenty recognized dynastic families have all been exhaustively researched by the Genealogical Office and by ancillary corroborative sources, Dr Edward MacLysaght, former Chief Herald in Dublin Castle, wrote in his *Irish Families:* 'There are few families about which there is more authentic information than the O'Donovans; not only do we have the officially verified pedigrees of the oldest branch from Gaelic times when they held a royal position, we have available the works of Dr John O'Donovan (1809-61), one of Ireland's most distinguished antiquarians.'

Dr O'Donovan once stated that he was perfectly comfortable with the authenticity of his scholarship back to the early centuries of the Christian era. But back beyond that period, he added, 'I would not want to carry any pedigree as I am very wary of the heady brew of fact, legend and myth.'

In the tenth century, one of the territorial kings, in what is now County Limerick, was Donndubhan ('dark headed'), son of the king of Munster, who gave his name to all succeeding Donovans. At the time of their expulsion in the mid-thirteenth century, the Chief of the O'Donovans had the personal nickname of An Crom, 'the stooped one', and was seventh in direct descent from Donndubhan. All O'Donovans of County Cork descend from An Crom.

The fortunes of the princely O'Donovans waxed and waned as the English/Anglo-Norman power in Ireland strengthened or declined. Several decades – even a century – of good times or bad for the old Gaelic nobles would often prevail until the rhythm of Irish history changed once more. Depending upon circumstances, the O'Donovans were stripped of titles and possessions – or rewarded and reinstated – as they co-operated with or rebelled against the new alien ascendancy.

Many O'Donovans were active Jacobites who shared the defeat and ruin of the Catholic King James II and fled to Europe as Wild Geese. Others played the political games astutely, switching allegiances and religious affiliations with aplomb – often with resounding success and at other times with disastrous, even fatal results. Brian Donovan, a scholar and historian from Wexford, has admiration for the adroit political moves of his noble ancestors: 'That the O'Donovan clan leaders survived the dramatic changes wrought during the sixteenth and seventeenth centuries is remarkable, but largely explained by their loyalty to the Crown and their willingness to adapt to English law, custom and governance. There were few Gaelic leaders who fared as well.'

Both The and Madam O'Donovan, reflect this duality of influence that threads its way through ancient and modern Irish history. The O'Donovan chiefs of the name, for example, have been Protestant for several centuries: Daniel O'Donovan's great-great-grandfather, the Reverend Morgan O'Donovan, was a rector of the Church of Ireland in Cork; his predecessor as chief, Richard O'Donovan, was a general in the British army serving in Spain and Flanders in the 1790s. Only a century previously, The O'Donovan was a colonel in James II's Catholic army fighting against the English. (With well-honed family political skill, however, the colonel avoided exile in Europe and The O'Donovan's estates were once more spared confiscation.)

Daniel O'Donovan's grandfather and father were senior officers in the British army who fought respectively in the Boer War in South Africa and in World War I. Both Jane's and Daniel's fathers were good friends serving together in the Royal Irish Fusiliers; Jane, at eighteen, often served as official hostess when her father, Field Marshall Sir Gerald Templer, KC, was high commissioner of Malaysia shortly before World War II.

The O'Donovan's intense pride of name also includes, very specially, the many courageous kinsman in more recent history who were distinguished patriots in the struggle for Irish independence from Great Britain.

The incumbent O'Donovan, born in France and educated at Stowe and Cambridge, lived in England working as an executive with an engineering company. Upon his mother's death in 1971, he inherited Hollybrook, a lovely 100-year-old residence and demesne of 200 acres, where he farms, gardens and restores lodges and stables on the estate for tourism purposes. The house – with its balconied grand hall, marquetry panelled library, colonnaded dining-room and reception rooms – is filled with historical, military and personal memorabilia including centuries-old battle trophies, daggers and shields, paintings, rare books and inscribed photographs of the Malaysian sultans with their courts.

The O'Donovans' three children live and work in London: Teige, the tanist, is a solicitor; Mary, a journalist, is married to the grandson of Britain's historically controversial prime minister, the late Neville Chamberlain; and Katherine, whose husband develops UK-Ukraine business opportunities, is an analyst with Credit Suisse.

Jane and Daniel O'Donovan are busy, vibrant people involved in local philanthropies and politics, Church of Ireland Synod affairs and representing the ancient family; in 1998 Daniel was elected Chairman of the Standing Council of Irish Chiefs.

About seven miles from Hollybrook House in Skibbereen and near the village of Drimoleague, is Castle Donovan, a former family seat. Built in 1560 on a ancient ceremonial site and later sacked by the Cromwellians, it stands as a monument to the survival of the dynasty. In June 2000 the chief of the name welcomed 1200 of his clansmen from around the world to a gathering at the ancient seat, the tall stark ruin, perched high on the sacred hill hauntingly silhouetted against the Carbery sky of West Cork. He later described the reunion of the noble clan as an extremely touching occasion.

In 1995 the O'Donovans donated Castle Donovan to the government of Ireland.

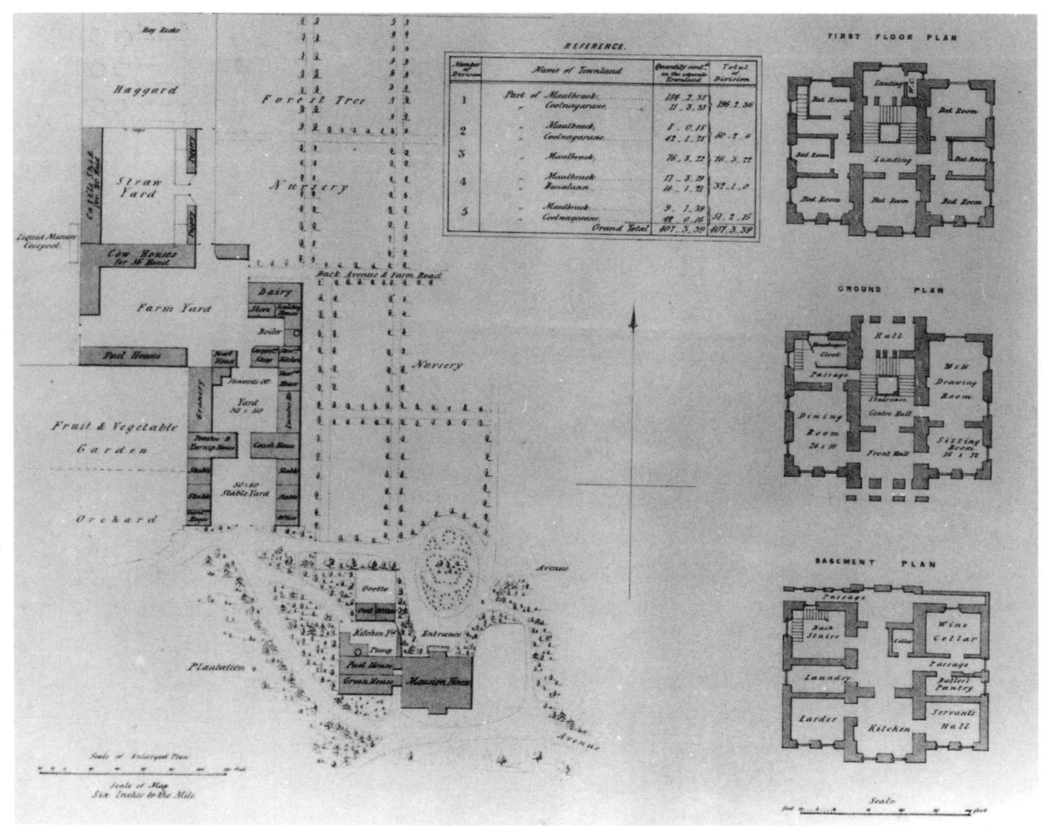


Plan and Elevation; Irish Architectural Archive

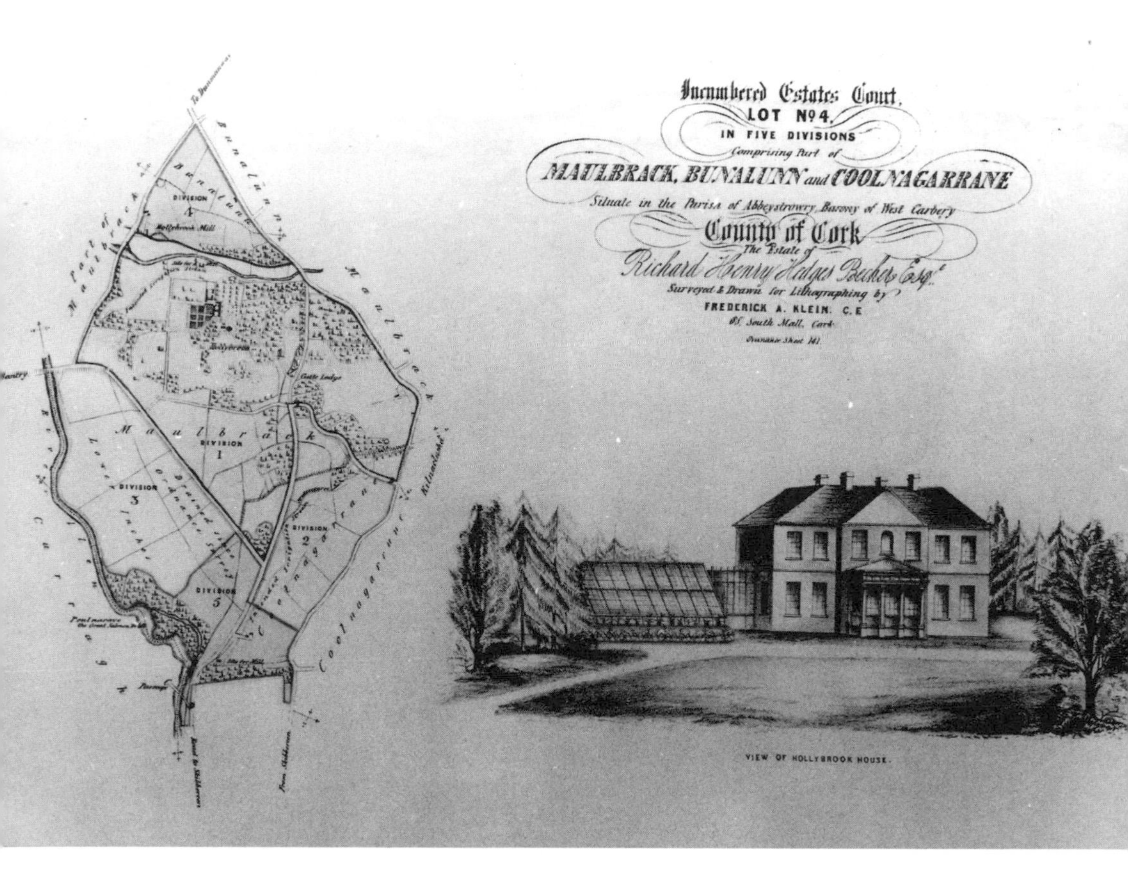

Incumbered Estates Court,
LOT No4,
IN FIVE DIVISIONS
Comprising Part of
MAULBRACK, BUNALUNN and COOLNAGARRANE
Situate in the Parish of Abbeystrowry, Barony of West Carbery
County of Cork
The Estate of
Richard Henry Hedges Becher Esqre
Surveyed & Drawn for Lithographing by
FREDERICK A. KLEIN. C.E
85 South Mall, Cork
DIVISION 4
Hollybrook Mill
Part of Maulbrack
Bunalunn
Maulbrack
Gate Lodge
DIVISION 1
DIVISION 3
DIVISION 2
DIVISION 5
Coolnagarrane
Road to Skibbereen
From Skibbereen
VIEW OF HOLLYBROOK HOUSE.

HOLLYBROOK HOUSE SKIBBEREEN, CO. CORK

GEOFFREY VINCENT PAUL O'DONOGHUE

# The O'Donoghue

## OF THE GLENS
## LORD OF GLENFLESK AND PRINCE OF LOUGH LEANE

Since the early Celtic migrations, the territory of the present-day County Kerry, one of the western-most regions of Europe, has received invaders, refugees and settlers who were drawn by its isolation and seduced by its beauty. Druid bards and modern travel writers alike have perceived Kerry as a wild, romantic area where the mountains meet the sea in dramatic fusion and vast moorland and pasture are dotted with a hundred silver loughs. In different ways throughout the centuries visitors have noted the special slanting light in south-western Munster that suffuses the landscape in a surreal aura. The O'Donoghues, however, came to Kerry not for its ambience, but for more pragmatic reasons: they were forced.

In the eleventh century the chiefly O'Donoghues (Donohoe, Donahue), originally from West Cork, were driven out of their historical homeland by their kin, the so called Eóghanacht MacCarthys, Kings of Munster and into Kerry where they eventually became very powerful. Although lords of their own domain in Kerry, the O'Donoghues prudently maintained a mutually beneficial feudal relationship with the MacCarthys – through marriage and pacts – and paid fealty to them as sovereigns of the province.

The O'Donoghue sept split into senior and cadet branches: The O'Donoghue Mór, with his seat at Ross Castle on Lough Leane; and his cousin, The O'Donoghue of the Glens, with his lands not far away at Glenflesk (Gleann Fleisce, i.e. Valley of the Hoops) in the Derrynasaggart Mountains, just south-east of the renowned range of MacGillycuddy's Reeks. The O'Donoghues – whose cohesive policy and strength of arms created an enduring clan dominance – controlled their territories as lords for over three hundred years.

Ross Castle, built in the fourteenth century on the shore of Lough Leane, the largest of the Killarney lakes, still stands surrounded by juniper, holly, mountain ash, sessile oak, eucalyptus and redwood trees. On a neighbouring peninsula separating the Muckross and Leane lakes there are yew woods, the oldest in Europe, dating back 10,000 years to the last Ice Age. The five-mile long Lough Leane and its thirty islands comprised the stronghold of the O'Donoghues; Ross Castle was its nucleus.

Having prevailed against adversaries for a dozen generations, Ross Castle was the last Gaelic stronghold in the kingdom of Munster to fall to Oliver Cromwell's army of Roundheads in 1652. In Killarney there is a famous legend that says the uneasy spirit of Donall, an O'Donoghue chief in the twelfth century, arises, on a silver-footed white horse, from Lough Leane at dawn on every first day of May to ride across the waters of the domain seeking the princely O'Donoghues. In 1984 all four stories of the castle were completely restored by the Irish Tourist Board. It serves as a silent reminder of the power and tenacity of the noble clan – and of Ireland's own resilience.

There is a consistent military element in the history of the O'Donoghues. From their forebear Conall Corc, King of Munster in the early Christian era (and common ancestor of the royal MacCarthys), to the present Chief, Geoffrey Vincent Paul O'Donoghue, who was born in 1937, service-in-arms has been a notable part of the princely family's tradition. Being natural enemies of the Anglo-Normans since the 1200s, the O'Donoghues survived the repeated turmoil of invasion and dispossession during the Tudor conquests (when the senior branch became extinct and The O'Donoghue of the Glens took the precedence), again during the Cromwellian confiscations and then again following the devastating defeat of the restored Stuart dynasty at the end of the seventeenth century when most of the aristocratic O'Donoghues went underground in their own homeland. The current O'Donoghue, a keen amateur historian, says that, although confiscations by the English were officially declared several times, The O'Donoghue and his family were able to retain the properties at Glenflesk because the fastness of the fortified Derrynasaggart valley always discouraged enforcement of English law.

A number of the O'Donoghues, who had served as officers in James II's star-crossed army, fled to a new life in exile after the Williamite victory at the Boyne in 1690 and were assimilated into the aristocratic ranks of several European societies. In the mid-1900s Florence O'Donoghue, son of the Chief, became a Chevalier of France and later Commander of the Body Guard for Queen Mary of Modena in Italy. A descendant cousin, Sean O'Donoghue, was a senior officer in the Irish Brigade of the Spanish army and, as hispanicized Lieutenant General Juan O Donojú (1755-1828), was appointed the last Spanish viceroy of Mexico.

In more recent generations, The O'Donoghue's predecessors went to Sandhurst for military training and served in the British and Irish armies. Geoffrey's ancestor and chiefly predecessor, Daniel O'Donoghue of the Glens was a member of Parliament (1857-83) at Westminster. Members of the clan also fought on both sides of the American Civil War. The incumbent O'Donoghue's father, Geoffrey Charles Patrick Randal, a Sandhurst graduate, had a turbulent military career. He was wounded and later court-marshalled and cashiered in France during World War I, where he served as a British army lieutenant; he went on to become a private in the South Irish Horse and then served as a lance-corporal and a private with the Royal Dublin Fusiliers in India before being sacked again. He finished his career as as a captain in the army of the newly created Irish Free State in the 1920s. The late Chief's problems stemmed from a combination of a truncated early home-life, unrecognized psychological consequences of 'shell-shock', alcohol and an intense personal dedication to Ireland's struggle for independence that had been fostered by his family's history.

The O'Donoghue's antecedents were rebels, plotters and leaders against the 'aliens from England'. In modern times they served in Dublin and in London as members of Parliament, high profile politicians, celebrated poets and clergymen of both faiths (principally Catholic). They have been successful bankers, railway executives, entrepreneurs, merchants and distinguished physicians. Whatever the occupation or period, The O'Donoghues have unfailingly played active roles in preserving their country's Gaelic identity and aristocratic traditions.

The O'Donoghue of the Glens, Lord of Glenflesk and Prince of Eóghanacht Loch Leane, Geoffrey Vincent Paul O'Donoghue, lives in a modern country house near Geashill, about six miles south-east of Tullamore in County Offaly. In the late 1800s his great-grandfather was the first of the chiefs to shift residence; for over five hundred years the seat of the O'Donoghues had been in Kerry. The current O'Donoghue – one of the many to be called Geoffrey (Séafraidh), a popular name for the family chiefs since the fourteenth century – carries on his legacy in the new region.

Geoffrey O'Donoghue is a widower whose young wife, Frances Kelly of Roscommon, a school teacher, was killed in 1984 by a speeding driver. He has raised their three sons and four daughters while managing the expansion of his successful farm equipment business.

Before The O'Donoghue first entered the business world as an aviation engineer with the British Aircraft Corporation, he followed his family's military bent by serving as a non-commissioned officer in the Irish Air Force. He had been educated in his earlier years at the Christian Brothers' School in Wexford and ran away to enlist in the Irish army at seventeen. Geoffrey is a mixture of ancient Gaelic Catholic nobility and the more recent Protestant Anglo-Irish gentry: The O'Donoghue's maternal great-grandfather was Sir John Ennis of Athlone and his mother's father was William Charlton of Clonmacnoise House, Offaly, former Surgeon-General of the British army.

The O'Donoghue, a proud parent and grandfather – six feet tall and erect with sandy hair trimmed short and a slightly tanned face – has the fitness of a footballer and the focus of an executive chairman. He applies much of his energy to his farm equipment enterprise, often working six days a week assisted by his family, associates and staff. He is also involved in Tullamore community affairs. An ancient county seat on the Grand Canal, Tullamore is an agriculturally prosperous centre with a famous whiskey distillery, brewery, sausage and bacon factory, worsted mill and highly productive pasture and meadowland. The monastery at Clonmacnoise is one of the many historically provocative features in the area.

History is a personal matter for Geoffrey O'Donoghue. Self-tutored as an historian and an Irish speaker, the Chief believes that the scope of Irish history is insufficiently known and inadequately taught in schools and even in universities. He feels that there is shallow knowledge of the great Gaelic period dominated in two millennia by the old dynastic order and no proper grasp of the lasting impact of the aristocratic traditions on the character of the land and its people.

The O'Donoghue says that if the average man or woman ever thinks about it all, they mention only the aristocratic leaders who fled to Europe after the Jacobite defeat in the seventeenth century, leaving behind the ordinary Irishmen to suffer under the Penal Laws. He feels there is a vague sort of mistaken impression among the ordinary citizens of Ireland that those so-called Wild Geese were, in a way, deserters .

Geoffrey O'Donoghue considers his own family's saga an example of the synergistic blend of aristocratic and patriotic traditions that characterized the past centuries of Gaelic ascendancy. Through public relations efforts by the Standing Council of Irish Chiefs and support from government agencies, along with renewed emphasis on improvement in teaching, The O'Donoghue hopes that Ireland's dramatic past can be more fully understood. He believes that as it is always the victors who write history, special slants and omissions are inevitable – but, in the end, they are intellectually unacceptable. The O'Donoghue does not, however, object to revisionism if it leads to historical accuracy.

ROSS CASTLE, KILLARNEY, CO. KERRY
From J. Fisher, *A picturesque Tour of Killarney*, 1789; Irish Architectural Archive

RICHARD DENYS WYER MCGILLYCUDDY

# The McGillycuddy

## OF THE REEKS

A 'reek' in Ireland rarely has an olfactory implication; it almost always means a mountain – a big one. Of Saxon origin ('hreach'), the word itself is more familiar in modern English as 'rick', meaning a stack, a pile of grain or wheat. Macgillycuddy's Reeks, one of the dominant features of County Kerry and the highest mountains in Ireland, stretch like enormous conical haystacks from Beaufort near Killarney, south to Glencar and the mouth of the Kenmare River. The loftiest point of the Reeks with their peaked and jagged summits is Carrauntoohil (3414 ft) approached through the Gap of Dunloe, a deep irregular defile leading up from the shadowy Leane Valley.

For the past two hundred years the Reeks have been identified with the Mac Giolla Mochuda, the Kerry sept who have dwelt for centuries at their slopes. While emigration and a more mobile modern life have partially dispersed the tribal cluster, the McGillycuddys are still very numerous in that broad south-western section of Munster.

The McGillycuddys, as a separate sept, emerged only in historically recent times, but, according to chronicler Donnacha O'Cairain, they extend back fifteen hundred years in recorded history – and, by anecdote, a further millennium. Until the sixteenth century, they were a cadet or junior branch of the royal Munster dynasty of O Sullivan (Súileabháin, the One-eyed or Hawk-eyed) whose centre of power was concentrated around Kenmare Bay in south Kerry. The McGillycuddy branch – known from antiquity as O Sullivans – controlled the Iveagh peninsula, referred to by modern travellers as the Ring of Kerry.

The cadet O Sullivans had traditionally sought spiritual protection from the seventh century St Mochuda, founder of Lismore Abbey, and as it was common for male children in the early centuries of Christianity in Ireland to be named as the saint's disciple (or 'giolla'), Giolla Mochuda, or eventually Gillycuddy, became a family name and a force of its own. In 1563 Conor Giolla Mochuda O Sullivan murdered his noble kinsman Donal O Sullivan for murky political reasons – and from that point in time Conor's descendants were a distinct line who used the patronymic Mac Giolla Mochuda/ Mc Gillycuddy.

The direct royal descent of The McGillycuddy through the senior House of O Sullivan Mór and back to the dynasty of King Súileabháin of Munster (AD 950) was acknowledged in the early 1600s by The MacCarthy Mór, the ru-rí of Desmond – a region to the east of the Reeks – who in turn owed allegiance to the rí rech of the province, the King of Munster. The MacCarthy granted The McGillycuddy the territorial lordship of Doonebo, an area of south-west Munster where they had already held strong influence for many generations.

The famous mountain range that forms the spine of Munster became, by common usage, inextricably associated with the family that held such sway in the region since the pre-Christian era. Local residents say that their ancestors boasted of the ruler's wealth and claimed proudly that the giant pyramidal reeks that towered over them had been The McGillycuddy's stacks of grain in the very ancient days of Ireland.

In the middle 1800s the chief of the name himself became known formally as The McGillycuddy of the Reeks. (The chiefly family bears the 'Mc' rather than 'Mac' prefix.)

Richard Denis Wyer McGillycuddy, the present Chief, was born in 1948 and has lived in Ireland, England and France. Tall and rugged with tousled chestnut hair, The McGillycuddy has a contagious sense of humour and an obvious appetite for life. Although The McGillycuddys, as chiefs of the name, lived and served in various regions of the world in a variety of capacities, the core of the family had always been Kerry – never far from the mountains they cherished.

Over a stretch of many generations the once vast estates of the family became diminished by a combination of politics, economics, injudicious financial management and the simple sale of property. While some land and possessions were reacquired intermittently in later generations, the bulk of the McGillycuddy properties – including Flesk Castle near Killarney and other estates – have been reduced to the area around Beaufort at the north end of the mountains where the new family seat, a mansion called The Reeks, was built in the late 1700s. The chiefs lived and farmed extensively there until 1985 when the estate was sold – ironically to a family called O'Sullivan, the tribe-of-origin of the Giolla Mochuda.

Like the famous reeks in their kingdom, the fortunes of the House of McGillycuddy had peaks and valleys during the turbulent periods of Irish-Anglo-Norman conflicts: as always, it depended on whether the family had joined the side whose power prevailed at the time. The noble line kept its genealogical integrity through the tenacity of the old Gaelic aristocratic tradition; and it survived as a solid part of the Anglo-Irish ascendancy by politically expedient alliances – and by luck. While the lordly O'Sullivan-McGillycuddys were heroic in their historical opposition to the Anglo-Norman incursion and, later, to its defining Protestantism, by the early eighteenth century the family had had many intermarriages with the 'alien stock' and had become mainly members of the Church of Ireland. Even as early as the mid-1600s, Donough McGillycuddy had married a Protestant bishop's daughter and was a colonel in the English army.

Military service has been a tradition with The McGillycuddy's family for three hundred years; a previous Richard was aide-de-camp to the Duke of Wellington; another served with Lawrence of Arabia; the present Chief's grandfather served as a colonel in the British army – and was also a signatory of the 1937 Constitution and a senator of the Irish Free State at the same time; the incumbent's father, John Patrick, died (at The Reeks in 1959) ultimately of wounds received gallantly as a major with the Northampton Yeomanry during World War II.

The McGillycuddy's Anglo-Irish identity in recent generations never detracted from the family's popular standing in their native territory of Kerry, nor in the newly independent Ireland. Members of this old aristocratic line have served Ireland with distinction as senators, local officials, educators, physicians and churchmen.

Richard McGillycuddy, his wife Virginia and their daughters Tara and Sorcha, born in 1985 and 1990, live in Bellmont House, in Ballinea near Mullingar, County Westmeath, which they rent from the Gaisford-Lawrence family. A big, square Georgian pile built two hundred years ago, with the traditionally spacious, comfortable and slightly tattered grandeur of patrician country houses in Ireland, Bellmont sits on flat fertile farmland – with not a hill in sight. The Reeks in Kerry was sold when his family lived in France. It was the passing of an era.

The current Chief – whose title was recognized by the Irish Free State in 1944 and acknowledged by the Republic in 1948 – was educated at Eton and at the University of Aix-en-Provence. He worked in Paris as an estate agent and investor for over a decade before returning to Ireland where he now farms the Westmeath land and is a property consultant. Richard McGillycuddy is also active in the Standing Council of Irish Chiefs and in clan affairs.

Madam McGillycuddy is the granddaughter of the first Baron Astor of Hever of Hever Castle in Kent and the eldest daughter of the Honourable Hugh Waldorf Astor, the Baron's second son. She is a first cousin of the Marquis Lansdowne, Earl of Kerry, whose FitzMaurice and FitzGerald forebears were the quintessential invaders opposed (and then married into) by the old Gaelic noble houses half a millennium ago. Virginia Astor McGillycuddy, a raven-haired beauty with dark eyes and a bright smile, is an excellent painter and a keen amateur historian. Her close American connections include her relative, Brooke (Mrs Vincent) Astor, the grande dame of New York City's social, cultural and philanthropic worlds, and her great-aunt, the late Diana Vreeland, editor-in-chief of *Vogue* and undisputed high priestess of fashion for decades before and after World War II.

The McGillycuddy's genealogy traces authentically to King Súileabháin/Sullivan over a thousand years ago. During the 1970s William Hennessy of the Royal Irish Academy in Dublin compiled the lineage back further to Oilill Olum, King of Munster, who died in AD 234. It is staggering to consider that historical epic oral tradition in Ireland – which is given reasonable credence by some respected scholars and genealogists – represents Oilill Olum as the forty-third direct descendent of Milesius, the King of Spain, whose sons reputedly came from the Iberian peninsula a millennium before the birth of Christ and were the progenitors of most of the ancient noble families in Ireland today.

Richard, The McGillycuddy of the Reeks sometimes says that his family has been in existence almost as long at the old stony hay-stacks in County Kerry.

THE REEKS, BEAUFORT, CO. KERRY
Courtesy Richard McGillycuddy

HENRY O'GRADY

# The O'Grady

## OF KILBALLYOWEN

It is a quantum psychic leap from Britain's financial centre to the woodlands and pastures of County Limerick – although the distance that separate these two realms is only 400 miles as the crow flies. Henry Thomas Standish The O'Grady, a bachelor born in Sussex in 1974, was, until 2002, a stockbroker in London's financial district; he often thinks, however, about the ancestral seat of The O'Grady – Kilballyowen, near the village of Bruff, about thirty minutes by car from Limerick City – where he has often visited but never lived. Ironically, Henry, the current bearer of the title, also may never possess the seat.

The O'Grady (Ó Grádaigh) clan originated in County Clare, although the seat and territory of the Chief has been at Kilballyowen for seven centuries. Henry's step-grandmother, the former Mollie McLean from Gibson Island, Maryland, the late Dowager Madam O'Grady (1929-2003), had lifetime use of Kilballyowen. Her husband, Gerald Vigors de Courcy The O'Grady (1912-93) – a former British army lieutenant colonel and aide-de-camp to the commander-in-chief in India before retiring to farm in Ireland – was succeeded by his tanist and only son, Brian de Courcy, Henry's father. Gerald also had three daughters: Catherine, by his first wife, Pamela Thornton of Brockhall, an English heiress from Northhampton; and Eliza and Faith, by Mollie McLean.

Brian The O'Grady, born in 1943, a senior insurance executive with Marsh McLennan in London, had been chief of the name for only five years when he died of cancer. He is survived by his widow, Madam O'Grady, the former Mary Bruning; his son Henry, the new Chief; and his daughter Olivia. Brian, educated, married, employed and resident in England, is buried in Colemans Hatch, the Sussex village where he had lived.

There are local people around Bruff who say that the O'Grady crypt and mausoleum at Knockany, as well as an O'Grady cousin's property eight miles away at Cappamore – and even Kilballyowen House itself – are haunted. When villagers are questioned about the ghosts that dog the family of the Chief, the locals usually smile or shrug, but do not dismiss the possibility.

Very old traditions persist in the noble O'Grady family; including the belief among some of them that spirits of the past revisit the O'Gradys from time to time. One ghostly experience persisted vividly in the memory of the late Dowager Madam O'Grady of Kilballyowen. In 1999 she recounted the following to the author as she walked the land that has been held by her late husband's family since two hundred years before Columbus discovered her home state, Maryland:

> The Kilballyowen O'Gradys were always keen fox-hunters, kept good horses and had a famous pack of hounds for generations. In the early 1800s one of my husband's predecessors was obsessed with hunting. Late one night, after a bad day in the field and maddened by whiskey – which I think he was also obsessed with – he went out to the kennels and whipped to death a dozen or more hounds. Ever since then, each time an heir of The O'Grady is expected at Kilballyowen, at some point before the birth, spectral hounds come at night to the pregnant wife of the Chief and, in a ghostly nightmarish attack, try to claw the unborn baby away. It happened to me – twice – over thirty years ago when we were still living in the big house and I was expecting Eliza and then later Faith (Henry's aunts). That was a shake-up for a quiet Vassar [College] girl from Gibson Island. There is a lot of old, strange history around here at Kilballyowen.

The O'Gradys, one of the most ancient families in north Munster or Thomond, shared power and common ancestry with The O'Briens a thousand years ago. The O'Briens, however, expanded their influence, particularly under the leadership of the extraordinary King Brian Boru and established themselves as the ascendancy power in that territory; they became the hereditary rulers of Thomond – and eventually of all of Ireland. The O'Gradys acknowledged the paramount sway of the O'Briens and held the dynastic chieftainship of the O'Grady clan under the protective provincial banner of their ancestral cousins, the O'Briens.

The O'Grady's were formidable warriors and, early on, strong defenders of the Church. Johannes O'Grady of Kilballyowen was Archbishop of Tuam in the late fourteenth Century. The family has owned the lands of Kilballyowen since 1301 when Hugh O'Grady married the daughter and heir of O'Kerwick, a neighbouring chief.

The Kilballyowen O'Gradys, like many other Gaelic dynasts, ultimately chose accommodation with the spreading Anglo-Norman force of arms and policy. In a mélange of coercion, co-operation and the contagious expedience of intermarriage, the O'Gradys eventually favoured the English invaders at the time of Henry VIII and were thereby able to retain their land and title. The O'Gradys of Kilballyowen have been Protestants since the eighteenth century and have produced a number of prominent Church of Ireland ministers. They have also fielded officers in the British army for several hundred years – including Henry's grandfather, Gerald.

With a genetic blend of Irish, Scottish, English and German blood (his maternal grandparents came to England from Germany two generations ago, a great-grandfather in Berlin having been the last Chancellor before Hitler), Henry The O'Grady feels strong pride – along with a certain wariness – about his predominantly Anglo-Irish legacy. From a materialistic standpoint, Henry, like his father, Brian, has seen two inheritances drastically eroded by economic recession and bad luck.

The increasingly unprofitable farming operations at Kilballyowen left Henry's proudly aristocratic, highly principled paternal grandfather, Gerald de Courcy O'Grady, frustrated and financially drained. In 1967, Gerald, in a fit of practicality untypical of his noble breed, tore down Kilballyowen House, the huge, cut-stone manor house dating from the late 1700s that had incorporated a much earlier O'Grady castle and built a small modern house in its stead. His daughters by Mollie inherited the house and demesne at her death.

A somewhat similar scenario exists several miles from Kilballyowen, between the hamlets of Pallas Green and Cappamore, at the property owned by David O'Grady Thompson, a relative of Henry O'Grady. His residence, Castlegarde, one of the longest continuously family-occupied castles in Ireland, is starkly dramatic with its weather-blackened exterior, crenellated roof, moat, chain-gate and the reputedly haunted tower section dating back to AD 1196; however, it is in perilous condition inside and out. The castle, pastures and gardens were flourishing before and after the halcyon days of David's recent ancestors, the Honourable Waller O'Grady, Queen's Counsel and his predecessor, Standish O'Grady, who was raised to the peerage in 1851 as Viscount Guillamore. (The title became extinct in 1955.)

David Thompson's father, Hugh, inherited Castlegarde from his aunt, Lady Guillamore, widow of the 9th viscount. As a cattle and sheep farmer, grain merchant and investor, Hugh Thompson suffered repeatedly from recessions in the agricultural sector, the stock market, plus his wife's fragile health and eventual death. The castle fell rapidly into disrepair, as Hugh closed off dozens of rooms and compressed his living quarters into a fraction of its former area. Three years after his father's death in 1998, David, with his wife Hazel and three children, agreed to move into the castle, which was headed for certain dilapidation and ruin: a courageous decision.

David O'Grady Thompson has gamely grasped the nettle. He left his management job at Ranks as an expert animal nutritionist and in 2000 began full dedication – funded by his new mushroom farming operation at Castlegarde, modest personal resources and a minor grant from the local government heritage council – to the restoration of this historic O'Grady castle for his family and for posterity.

Henry The O'Grady, went to Harrow, Bristol University and has a second Masters degree from Oxford. He is a member of the Standing Council of Irish Chiefs and has nominated his first cousin, Donagh, who farms at Askeaton, County Limerick, as his tanist. Henry, who speaks French, worked in Paris for a management consulting company and then for an American brokerage firm in London. In 2003, he worked in the Caribbean for an English firm, organizing sponsorship for West Indian cricket and also serving as a commentator on Guyanan television. The O'Grady likes international business and foresees his future in it.

The ghosts of Kilballyowen, nevertheless, perhaps sometimes visit his dreams and remind him that, as chief of the name, his place is there. They may also suggest that perhaps the vast, tottering but still standing stone stables, last used in his father's childhood, as well as the farm staff housing, the kennels and outbuildings of Kilballyowen could, like Castlegarde, be restored for a practical purpose; and that perhaps some unforeseen circumstance might occur that could allow Henry to return eventually to the seat and legacy of The O'Grady of Kilballyowen.

KILBALLYOWEN HOUSE, BRUFF, CO. LIMERICK
Irish Architectural Archive

DENIS CLEMENT LONG
AND HIS WIFE, LESTER LONG

# The O'Long

## OF GARRANELONGY
## LORD OF CANOVEE

Denis Clement Long – The O'Long (Ó Longaidh) of Garranelongy and Lord of Canovee – was born in Cork in 1930. He has the demeanour of a scholar and the precision of a CEO – attributes well-earned by this scion of the princely Long family and fortieth in direct male descent from Oengus, the first Christian king of Munster (d. AD 492). The O'Long, a low-key gentleman who favours Dublin-tailored tweed suits, has the compact build and easy carriage of a veteran sportsman. He, his wife, the former Lester Jean O'Rorke Clarke and their two sons live quietly in a two-storey Georgian House built in the late 1700s on a small bluff one hundred yards above the principal road from Farnanes to Bandon in County Cork, the area where successive O'Long chiefs of the name were hereditary lords for centuries.

For thirty-five years, The O'Long was Chief Executive of the Blarney Pigs Company and the D.C. Long Co., Ltd of Cork where his son and tanist, James, born in 1973, educated at University College Cork, serves as a director. James's younger brother, Oliver, studied horticulture at the Department of Agriculture College and qualified as a horticulturist in 1998.

The and Madam O'Long are entrenched happily in the traditional territory of Muskerry, lands through which the river Lee flows – the areas of Canovee, Moviddy, Kilbonane, Kilmurry and Dunsky. Indeed, Ó Longaidh were rulers before the Anglo-Normans invaded Ireland in the twelfth century. Lester Long, a calm, pretty woman, smiles when she quietly refers to the continuity and endurance of the old territorial nomenclature and mentions how her husband, the incumbent Chief, is closely involved with local organizations still bearing names redolent of Muskerry and Cork history: The

O'Long hunts with the Muskerry Hounds, and is honorary secretary of the Canovee Historical and Archeological Society and the Kilmurry Historical Society.

In addition to his prominence as a successful businessman and keen foxhunter, Denis Long has a wide reputation as a pro-active supporter of Gaelic culture and the Irish language; he is an author and lecturer in history – national, local and family – and is a council member of the Cork Historical and Archeological Society.

From the time St Patrick baptized King Oengus at Cashel in the fifth century, the Longs have been unwaveringly Roman Catholic – a dangerous dedication in light of the political violence that accompanied such loyalty through much of Irish history.

Most of the Longs did not flee to Europe after the defeat of the Catholic King James II (although some had fought bravely at Kinsale with the Jacobites' Spanish allies against the victorious forces of the Dutch prince, William of Orange). From the outset, in the sixteenth century, Longs had resisted the Elizabethan conquest, suffered consequences, but later received pardons and were able to retain their position – until the next cycle. This to-and-fro behavioural pattern weaves its way through the family's history: resistance, pardon, re-establishment, rebellion, concession, recovery.

The title and territorial lordship of The O'Long was abolished at the time of the Chief's feudal submission to the English monarch after the collapse of James II's campaign; in exchange, certain lands were returned to the family by the Crown. A decade later, his patent of nobility restored, The O'Long was granted permission to build a family seat, the manor of 'Mount Long' that still stands near Oysterhaven, Cork and is now owned by the Irish State. In the mid 1600s, at the Restoration (of the Catholic King Charles II of England), the ancient Muskerry lands had also been returned to The O'Long along with the estate of Canovee, site of the ancestral family seat called Garranelongy (Grove of the Longs), confiscated earlier by the English settlers and renamed Bellmount.

The O'Longs, chiefs of the name, were able, through centuries of challenge, to prevail. Courage, luck, agility – perhaps the fortuitous marriages into the powerful Anglo-Norman families of the FitzGeralds and the Butlers in the 1700s – all were part of the Longs' recipe for survival as aristocrats and as Roman Catholics.

In the last two hundred years Denis Clement Long's predecessors have included judges, high-sheriffs, counsellors and physicians; his father was a surgeon. Although Catholic and resolutely Irish, the Longs have also been, in the more recent historical era, supportive of the British Crown and of the concept of the Commonwealth. Denis Long, as chief of the name, is, however, proudly protective of his genealogical authenticity. He treats his own family documentation, along with ongoing professional research and the official recognition by the Chief Herald, with great respect and care. While certain additional documents of lineage are still being sought, Long bridles at any question of the integrity of the linkage to the ancient origins of his surviving Gaelic clan and to his direct ancestor, King Oengus of Munster.

A participating member of the Council of Irish Chiefs and an expert in Irish history, Denis Long admires and supports the Brehon system of tanistry

The O'Long has a wistful yet positive view on the subject of the old princely families. He notes that the existence of the Irish chiefs, as well as the continued survival of their dynasties, is virtually unknown to most Irish people today and he hopes that this will not always be the case.

MOUNT LONG CASTLE, CO. CORK
From Daniel Grose (c. 1776–1838), *The Antiquities of Ireland*, 1991;
Irish Architectural Archive

# LEINSTER

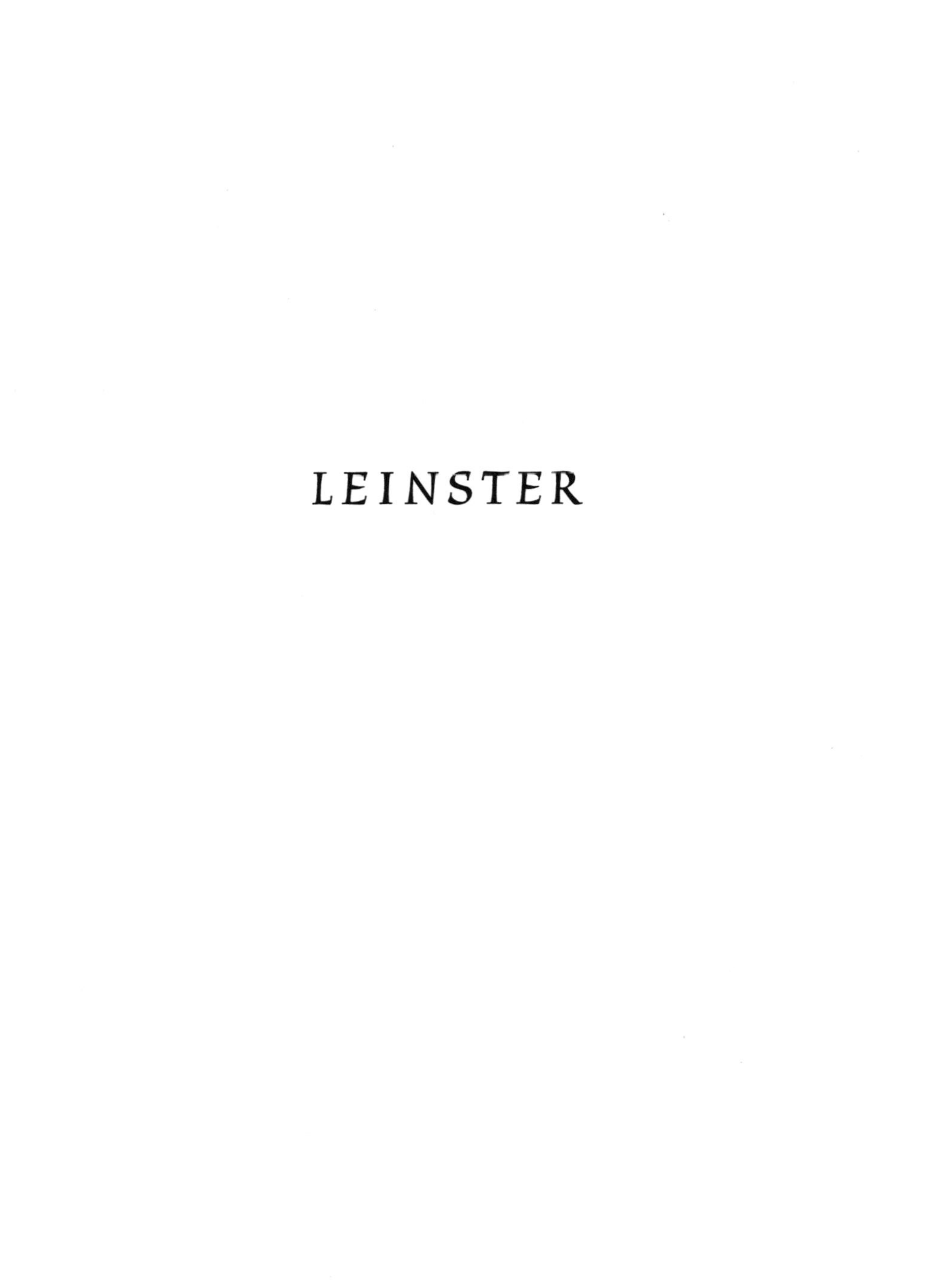

DOUGLAS JOHN FOX

# The Fox

## (AN SIONNACH)

Among the twenty officially recognized descendant chiefs of the princely Gaelic families, Douglas John Fox lives furthest away from the ancestral territories that his forebears ruled for centuries. The Fox has been established in Australia for three generations – eight thousand miles from the modern County Offaly (formerly King's County) once the heartland of his family's hereditary realm.

There is also a wide separation of attitudes between the incumbent Fox and most of his chiefly peers: Douglas is singularly casual about his aristocratic Fox legacy; he accepts his position as the legitimate lineal heir to the ancient Gaelic title, chief of the name, as meaningful but quite far removed from the centre of his life. Douglas Fox owns and operates a popular delicatessen in Mildura, Victoria.

The family of The Fox were chiefs and petty kings long before the Christian era – and long afterwards. They descend from the Milesian progenitors whose offspring later established, among other dynasties, the kingship of Teffia in Leinster, which ultimately included portions of present day counties Meath, Westmeath and Offaly.

In the early centuries of Christianity in Ireland, the family became known as Ó Kearney or Carney (in the anglicized form) from their chief, Tadgh Ó Catharnaigh (d. 1084). King Tadgh's extraordinary cunning had earned him the nickname, 'An Sionnach', i.e. The Fox. In due course, the Ó Catharnaigh branch acquired the sobriquet as a distinct surname; since the English language was first introduced into Ireland, the head of the family has been called The Fox – and is deemed authentic by the Genealogical Office in Dublin.

(The English settlers of the name Fox – some of whom became extensive landlords in County Limerick – are not related to the old Gaelic family of The Fox.)

By the thirteenth century the Kingdom of Teffia had been overpowered and partitioned by rival Gaelic monarchs; for several generations the Foxes' ranking in the power structure gradually declined from king to prince and eventually to lord of a designated region. As their fortunes waned, The Foxes clung tenaciously for hundreds of years to what remained. Even when their influence had diminished they still retained considerable territory in Offaly and became Barons of Kilcoursey. Further shrinkage of their former sway and their possessions occurred in the sixteenth century during the Tudor period with the expansion and tightening of the English grip on Ireland.

Although The Fox and his clan had initially resisted English force, they ultimately bent to the conquest. They co-operated with the entrenched invader, accepted the conquerors' blandishments – even embracing (or at least assuming) – the anglican faith. Hubert The Fox surrendered the Barony of Kilcoursey to Queen Elizabeth I in 1595 and had it promptly regranted to him and his male heirs under subordinating conditions. Forty years later the bulk of the remaining Fox territories were seized once again and distributed to the Earl of Cavan, a royalist English settler called Lambart.

Through rebellions, peace agreements and uprisings there were losses, gains and more losses as The Foxes dealt with history over the ensuing generations. By the end of the seventeenth century, their royal prerogatives and possessions were mostly reduced to memories and distilled into clan lore; the title of The Fox, however, secretly passed within the family – always in accordance with the Brehon Laws of succession.

Over dozens of generations and into the twentieth century, the family of The Fox became staunchly Protestant Irish gentry – steadfast, nevertheless, in their respect for the title of The Fox and all the ancient traditions it represents.

Since the eighteenth century the Foxes have produced farmers, anglican clergymen, British army officers, businessmen, doctors and justices. Most of the family have remained in Ireland, dispersed throughout the Republic, with a cluster still on their ancestral lands. In 1959 the title shifted to Australia.

Douglas John The Fox, who was born in Mildura, Victoria in 1942 and attended St Joseph's School, still lives and works in Mildura, a medium-sized country town 345 miles by highway from Melbourne. The area, though naturally arid, has effective irrigation enabling good commercial production of fruit and nuts and there is a bustling business community whose tastes have created a robust business for Douglas Fox's delicatessen, where he often works sixteen hours a day, including weekends. He and his wife Marjorie Adeline have three daughters and a son, Gary John (b. 1964), who is The Fox's tanist.

Neither Douglas nor his father, John William Fox (b. 1916), have ever been to Ireland; both want very much to visit the land of their origins. Douglas' great-grandfather, Brassil Fox (1844-1913) emigrated from Ireland and settled in New South Wales, Australia. Brassil's son, James George Fox (1873-1937), Douglas' grandfather (well-known as Jimmy Fox in Australian racing circles), won the Adelaide Sweepstakes – a clear indication, the newspapers said, of the Fox Irish genes.

John William The Fox of Koorlong, Victoria, was a poultry farmer before his retirement. Born in Tempe and educated at the Gidson State School, his life centred on his wife and five children. When Madam Fox died in 1997 and his own health faltered, John decided to abdicate his hereditary position: he used the Brehon system of approval by the three generation family radius to pass the title of The Fox to his son Douglas John in 1998.

The incumbent chief of the name is totally and proudly Australian. He does not disregard his family's role in Ireland's past, nor his own surviving designation as The Fox. His perspectives, however, are quite unlike those of most of his fellow chiefs.

Douglas John The Fox is firmly informal. He has the build of a middleweight prize-fighter, steely eyes, a straight nose and short brown hair; a tie and a jacket would be uncommon garb. A quiet, private man, Douglas Fox has a sharp mind and a warm nature, possibly prickly if pressed.

After being members of the Church of Ireland for five hundred years, The Fox and his immediate family are once again Roman Catholic. Douglas admits to scant knowledge of Irish affairs and has not taken his seat on the Standing Council of Irish Chiefs. The banner of this descendant of the kings and princes of Teffia hangs in the Heraldic Museum in Dublin – unseen, as yet, by the previous and present chiefs of the name – Douglas and his father.

Today, The Fox, by virtue of his location as well as his temperament, is probably one of the least known and most diffident members of Ireland's well-hidden Gaelic aristocracy.

*Galtrim House,* overleaf, *built in the early nineteenth century, is associated with The Foxes. The family lived here from the 1820s to the 1930s*

GALTRIM HOUSE, DUNSANY, CO. MEATH
Courtesy Eileen, Lady Mountcharles

DAVID O'MORCHOE

# The O'Morchoe

## OF OULARTLEIGH

O'Morchoe (Ó Murchu, Ó Murchada: 'spawn of the sea-hound and warrior') is more familiarly known in the anglicized form as Murphy, the most common name in Ireland – more than 1 per cent of the current total population. Usage of the O'Morchoe form (pronounced 'o-murroe'), an old, otherwise obsolete name in English, is limited today to the immediate kin of the chief of the name. Although Murphy is much the commonest surname, the incumbent Chief of this princely house, David Niall Creagh The O'Morchoe, is a most uncommon man.

Descended from the ancient kings of Leinster, David O'Morchoe (b. 1928) lives near the town of Gorey in County Wexford, the traditional clan territory in the south-eastern section of the country. He and his wife, the former Margaret Brewitt of Cork, have three children: Maureen (b. 1964), an occupational therapist married to a computer technician; Dermot (b. 1956), the tanist, a commercial mushroom producer and horticulturist; and Kevin, an agriculturalist turned accountant. Another daughter died in childhood. The O'Morchoes are an attractive, relaxed couple, and a dynamic partnership. They have lived in Europe, Africa and the Middle East. The O'Morchoe, now a sheep farmer, is a former major general in the British army.

Two of David O'Morchoe's uncles, Arthur and Kenneth and his father, Nial Creagh O'Morchoe (who succeeded his uncle Arthur as Chief) served in World War I in the Leinster Regiment, which was disbanded on the formation of the Irish State. Arthur served in the Colonial Service until retiring to farm in County Wexford during World War II. David's father joined the Indian Army and Kenneth served in the Gordon Highlanders. They had distinguished careers before retiring back to Ireland after the war. At the time of his father's death in 1970, David had been in the army for twenty-four years.

The O'Morchoe was commissioned into the Royal Irish Fusiliers from the Royal Military Academy, Sandhurst in 1948. He served in the Suez Canal Zone, Aqaba, Gibraltar and Germany before seconding for a three year attachment with the Parachute Regiment, which had been sent to the Suez Canal Zone. He returned to the Royal Irish Fusiliers in 1956 and served in Kenya towards the end of the anti-Mau Mau operations. He commanded the 1st Battalion of the Royal Irish Fusiliers in 1967/68 and, after a period on the directing staff of the British Army Staff College, he commanded the 16th Parachute Brigade Group. While in that post, O'Morchoe undertook a major NATO exercise under the command of the 82nd (US) Airborne Division in Turkey having first visited Fort Bragg, South Carolina on a co-ordinating visit.

Before his retirement in 1979, this much decorated professional soldier had the extraordinary responsibility of being commander-in-chief of the army of the Sultan of Oman. Among his other official recognitions for merit – both British and foreign – Major General O'Morchoe holds an MBE (Member of the Order of the British Empire) and a CB (Companion of the Order of the Bath).

Both Margaret and David O'Morchoe relished the military life with its peaks and valleys of contentment and its sense of accomplishment. The life of an army officer's wife, under any circumstances, says the general, demands stamina and patience; Madam O'Morchoe, he points out, whether based in Ireland, Britain, or abroad, raised their children, supervised staff, entertained guests, became affiliated with local civic and philanthropic bodies and served as an essential source of support, guidance and affection for her husband on their various tours of duty. They recall with pleasure their last post; they very much liked the Omani people as well as the Sultan and his family and found the intricate swirl of politics in that area of the Persian Gulf fascinating.

General O' Morchoe says that life in Ireland in the mid-1940s for a young person was 'narrow and very segregated'; the Catholic and Protestant communities kept much to themselves. Following two members of his immediate family into a military career, he says, broadened his horizons. He remembers, however, feeling – as an Irishman – quietly uncomfortable being in the (British) army during the very difficult period of violence and unrest in the 1970s in Northern Ireland.

Historically, the O'Morchoes were more than uncomfortable with the English and Norman foreigners; for centuries the royal house of Leinster fought fiercely against the invaders. These Gaelic nobles held their ground, along with their territorial authority, until the sixteenth century when Donal Mór The Ó Morchoe of Oulartleigh agreed to submit to Henry VIII – by anglicizing his religion as well as his name – in exchange for permission to retain his patent of nobility and for allowing the newly conformed 'Daniel Murphy' and his descendants to live peacefully in Wexford.

All was lost once again, however, when the family joined the unsuccessful Irish rebellion against the English a hundred years later.

Whatever the vicissitudes of the old Gaelic aristocracy under the conquering aliens, the family of The O'Morchoe of Oulartleigh, even as nominally anglicized 'Murphys', remained unshakably Irish – and, in the later centuries, staunchly Protestant. In the 1850s the clan lands at Oulartleigh finally passed out of the family due to the insolvency of the then Chief. Arthur Murphy, in the mid-1800s had re-established the family pedigree and title, which had been nullified by English law three centuries earlier and asserted his legal right to be called O'Morchoe of Oulartleigh. Arthur's son, the Reverend Thomas MacMurrough Murphy, rector of the Church of Ireland in Kiltermain, County Dublin and great-grandfather of the present Chief, went a step further: in 1895 he officially changed his name, by deed poll, back to O' Morchoe.

As with all of the old Gaelic dynastic families, it is difficult for a contemporary historian to grasp the staggering antiquity of The O'Morchoe's line whose roots reach back to King Dermot MacMurrough of Leinster in the twelfth century; and are traceable from Dermot to King Ughaine who, according to mythological and pseudo-historical traditions, was the fifty-ninth successor to Milesius of Spain, progenitor of the Gaels themselves in Ireland.

When David O'Morchoe retired to Ireland there was still considerable unrest in the North; for security reasons, although he and his family were well known in Gorey, where he had retired, he did not use his rank. He and his family integrated well into the local community, many of whom knew him from his late childhood.

The and Madam O'Morchoe love their 250-year-old house, Ardgarry, in the townland of Ballinacarrig near Gorey, a market-town about twenty miles from St George's Channel and the Irish Sea. The long, originally one-storey farm house, beside a wide stream, was owned by David O'Morchoe's childless aunt – who during his absence from Ireland in the military – added second and third storeys, built massive stone walls, planted extensive lawns, trees and gardens and created, in the words of her own diary, 'a place suitable to a Chief and his family since all the other O'Morchoe properties are long gone'.

For eighteen months David O'Morchoe worked for a development agency called Concern Universale, of which he is still a Council Member, before returning to Gorey to farm his land and breed sheep for the market. He was a founder member of a lamb producer group that encourages lamb farmers to improve quality through breeding. His elder son Dermot has joined him to add commercial mushroom farming to their enterprise.

The O'Morchoe, a member and former Chairman of the Standing Council of Irish Chiefs and Chieftains, considers the remaining chiefs and their families to be of great historical interest even though they play no official role in modern Ireland.

In retirement he also takes a keen interest in the veterans of his old regiment and in the Royal British Legion, of which he is president in the Republic of Ireland. The latter is a membership organization that looks after ex-British servicemen living in Ireland who have fallen on hard times. The interest in his regiment, which comprised men from all over Ireland, led The O'Morchoe to become a member of the Military Heritage of Ireland Trust, dedicated to the encouragement of research into Ireland's military history, i.e. wherever Irishmen fought and for (or against) whomever. It is an all-Ireland trust that encourages meetings between those with a military interests and connections on both sides of the border, to meet.

The O'Morchoe continues in the leadership traditions of his dynasty.

*The view opposite is from the centre of the O'Morchoe clan land, which stretched from Enniscorthy east to the sea and then north to the Ounabarra River. The Blackstairs Mountains in the background and beyond was the territory of the MacMurrough Kavanaghs. The last land owned by the chiefs went from the family during the 1850s.* [D O'M]

LOOKING WEST FROM OULART HILL, CO. WEXFORD
Courtesy The O'Morchoe

WILLIAM BUTLER
MACMORROUGH KAVANAGH

ANDREW
MACMORROUGH KAVANAGH

# The MacMorrough Kavanagh

## OF BORRIS
## PRINCE OF LEINSTER

The title of The MacMorrough Kavanagh of Borris (MacMurchadha Caounhanach) was officially recognized by the Genealogical Office of the Government of Ireland in 1958 but a specific family member's name was not formally added to the Register of Chiefs until 1998. William Butler Kavanagh, the current MacMorrough Kavanagh of Borris, who was born in Wales in 1944 and lives there at the time of this writing, takes seriously his position as chief of the name of this ancient line of Leinster princes. Dynastic family histories, however – like the history of Ireland itself – can be intriguingly complex. Even under the scholarly light and stringent rules of the Genealogical Office, shadows of doubt regarding inheritance occasionally arise and linger privately in the minds of those concerned.

While William Butler Kavanagh's claim to the noble chieftainship was officially acknowledged and his application for membership in the Standing Council of Irish Chiefs was submitted in 2000, a kinsman has a nagging question that persists in his mind: Does William Butler Kavanagh hold the title rightly? Andrew MacMorrough Kavanagh of Borris (b. 1948) poses the question rhetorically and quietly, but just as seriously as his distant cousin William takes his chieftainship

MacMorrough Kavanagh of Borris is one of the most illustrious names in Ireland. Descended from the rulers of Leinster, the easternmost of the provinces – who were kings down to the reign of Henry VIII of England and then provincial ruling princes well into modern history – the family was at the heart of Irish historical events for centuries. Their ancestor Dermot

MacMorrough (1110-71), King of Leinster, sought help from the King of England, Henry II, against the serious threat of the Viking Norsemen. To assist Dermot, Henry sent Richard FitzGilbert de Clare, the Earl of Pembroke, known as Strongbow, with a well trained, well armed force, a gesture that became the immediate cause of the ultimately devastating Anglo-Norman invasion. Two hundred years later, Dermot's descendent Art MacMorrough (1357-1417), also King of Leinster, partly counteracted his great-great-grandfather's vital harm to Gaelic Ireland: by his continuous and successful resistance to English aggression he did much to remove the opprobrium and hatred that had become attached to the family name.

The names Kavanagh and MacMorrough (the former being an ancient branch of the MacMorroughs) have been linked since the eleventh century. Their principal territories are now counties Wexford and Carlow where many still have influence and standing. Since medieval times the MacMorrough Kavanaghs were in positions of power on both sides of the relationship between Ireland and England and produced a kaleidoscope of opposing affiliations, successes, failures and larger-than-life characters.

Among the noble MacMorrough Kavanaghs there were monarchs, princes, soldiers, rebels, statesmen and jurists. They were fighters in the Geraldine (i.e. FitzGerald) rebellion against the English in the 1500s; a century later Brian Kavanagh, The MacMorrough, one of the many of his family who fought as Jacobite officers for the Stuart cause, was known as the tallest man in King James I's army. Brian's successor as chief of the name was Morgan Kavanagh of Borris whose son Charles became a general in the Austrian army and rose to be Governor of Prague in 1766. Evidently carrying his grandfather Brian's genes, Charles was described as the biggest man in Europe. Morgan's great-grandson Walter (d. 1813) was succeeded as chief by his brother Thomas who fought valiantly in Wexford against the English in the 1798 insurrection and was nicknamed by the local people as 'the monarch' – a salute to his royal Leinster blood as well as to his valour.

Both ironically and predictably, the MacMorrough Kavanaghs later fought equally valiantly under the banners of the invaders. Having conformed in the eighteenth century to the anglican 'Established Church' and having made expedient marital and political alliances, successive chiefs in modern times have been officers in the British army in the Boer War and World Wars I and II. Sir Dermot MacMorrough Kavanagh was equerry to both King George VI of England and to his daughter, Queen Elizabeth II.

Another distinguished clan member, the Right Honourable Arthur The MacMorrough Kavanagh of Borris (1831-1908), High Sheriff of counties Kilkenny and Carlow, member of the Irish Parliament and father of five, was born with only rudimentary stumps for arms and legs. In spite of his daunting disability Arthur became well able to shoot, fish and paint. He travelled extensively to Europe and Asia – and rode to hounds while strapped to his special saddle, taking the jumps in his stride. The saddle rests today in the library at Borris House in the care of his great-great-grandson Andrew MacMorrough Kavanagh.

The House of the MacMorrough Kavanagh, over a span of half a millennium reaching down to the mid-twentieth-century, married into the highest ranks of the powerful Anglo-Norman nobility in Ireland – FitzGeralds (Dukes of Leinster), Butlers (Marquesses of Ormond), le Poer Trench (Earls of Clancarty) – occasionally marrying into the same family several times in different centuries. The most recent example was the mother of Andrew MacMorrough Kavanagh of Borris, daughter of Major Arthur MacMorrough Kavanagh, chief of the name, who in 1936 married one of the ducal FitzGeralds. The niggling doubt in Andrew MacMorrough Kavanagh's mind about the chieftainship now held by William Butler Kavanagh is not basically fed by any personal animosity growing out of the feeling that the title should rightly be his. Nor does Andrew doubt the integrity of the Genealogical Office's research of the matter carried on for decades. The question arises out of the events of almost fifty years ago and the judgment of the then Chief Herald that followed in the circumstances.

Historian and Celtic scholar Peter Berresford Ellis, commented on the situation in his book, *Erin's Blood Royal* :

> The Chief Herald, Gerald Slavin, gave 'courtesy recognition' to a new MacMorrough Kavanagh in 1958 after the senior (Borris) line had ended without male heirs in primogeniture terms. Curiously, the Genealogical Office advised no one of this recognition. The new Chief's name was not inserted on the Clár na dTaoiseach (The Register of Chiefs) implying that the line was dormant since 1958 – as *Burke's Introduction to Irish Ancestry* had claimed in its 1976 edition. This omission and the accompanying silence allowed two lobbies to emerge – one supporting the son of a daughter of the penultimate chief, Major Arthur Thomas MacMorrough Kavanagh, who died in 1953 and the other supporting an elected head of a separate Kavanagh clan society. It was only in 1998, forty years after the first recognition that the Genealogical Office finally agreed to register William Butler Kavanagh's name …

Supporting their kinsman, the junior line – upon the death of Arthur who had four daughters – had applied immediately to the Chief Herald of Ireland to have their pedigree confirmed. No formal application of the tanistry principle seemed to have occurred. Their candidate was William Butler Kavanagh (b. 1944) whose father, also William Butler Kavanagh, had been born in 1914 in Springfield, Massachusetts (although the certificate of birth at the Registry of Vital Records held by the City Clerk in the city of his birth records the name as William Kevin Butler). The lobbying began.

The current chief of the name was born in Pembrokeshire, South Wales in 1944. He graduated from Shenstone College, a local school and became an engineer in the petroleum industry. His father had been raised in Scotland, his maternal homeland and trained at the University of St Andrews to be a civil engineer before moving to Wales where he served as the Pembroke Borough Surveyor. William, the incumbent Chief since 1962, has lived in Pembroke since childhood.

William and his Welsh wife, Margaret Joy Phillips, have two sons – Simon (b. 1967) and William Butler III (b. 1974). Simon, appointed tanist, has followed his father into the oil business and he worked as an engineer before commencing studies at Trinity College Dublin. William II, now retired, attends to matters regarding the Name while he and Madam MacMorrough Kavanagh divide their lives between their homes in Wales and in Florida.

William Butler The MacMorrough Kavanagh, a stocky man with a high, wide forehead, aviator-style glasses and a grey-flecked beard, is not oblivious to the discussions about his title – nor apathetic about the four decades it took, without official explanation, to get the family's name onto the Registry of Chiefs. He acknowledges that his claim to the Chieftainship is based on being the senior surviving line of the royal house – and he stresses that Brehon Law does not expressly exclude such a claim; it can be considered 'unopposed primogenital succession by passive tanistry'.

William and his immediate family are thinking about moving to Ireland from Wales, or at least about establishing a presence there. Indeed, his grandson Simon has already done so after a fashion; he completed his finals at Trinity College Dublin in the spring of 2004. Simon is an articulate advocate for his grandfather's position:

Simon told the author that:

> During the 1970s the MacMorrough Kavanagh chiefship was recorded as dormant – an utterly incorrect determination due probably to an inaccuracy in the book *The Irish Chiefs* [New York 1974] by Eugene Swezy. The error was carried forward into *Burke's Family Records, 1976* and repeated elsewhere – a source of irritation and embarrassment to my family.

William Butler Kavanagh's distant cousin Andrew MacMorrough Kavanagh and his wife Tina Murray, who has bloodlines in Dublin, Northern Ireland and Scotland, live in Borris House in the town of Borris, County Carlow, about forty miles north of Waterford and the Celtic Sea and the same distance west of St George's Channel in the Irish Sea. They and their five children, Morgan, Eleanor, Aoife, Alice and Rolline, do not plan to move anywhere. The MacMorrough Kavanaghs have been at the Borris House seat for over five hundred years.

The house – a huge square building of hand-hewn stone blocks – sits at the end of an avenue lined with oak trees, overlooking the woods and pastures of the ancient demesne; it demands constant attention. Andrew, trim and youthful in his mid-fifties, is a former professional jockey who also manages the farming activity with Tina and his son Morgan, a horse trainer. He considers Borris House an inherited responsibility – and a priority among tasks. On the south, west and east fronts of the house there are sixty-two windows both sides of which are flanked by the heads of different kings and queens of Leinster carved into the stonework.

Borris House was referred to as the 'old castle' in the mid-1600s and was incorporated into the house as different add-ons and extensions were made in the seventeenth, eighteenth and nineteenth centuries. Andrew does not plan on any additions: maintenance and repair are his current priorities.

Tina MacMorrough Kavanagh (b. 1951), an ebullient, attractive lady with light brown hair and quick movements, is a full partner in the Borris House activities. A graduate of Trinity College Dublin and, she says demurely but proudly, 'a former student demonstrator at the US embassy in Dublin against American policy in Vietnam', she shares a continuing curiosity about the succession to the family's princely title; Tina's interest, however, may be more activist and less academic than Andrew's; to her it is an ongoing topic that could ultimately be resolved – conceivably in their favour.

Andrew's grandfather, Arthur MacMorrough Kavanagh (1888–1953), The MacMorrough of Borris, a major in the 7th Queen's Own Hussars, had four daughters and no sons. Joane, his eldest (b. 1915), was married to Gerald, the Marquess of Kildare and only child of the 7th Duke of Leinster and had three daughters by him. After her divorce in 1946, Joane married Lieutenant Colonel Archibald Macalpine-Downie, a British army officer; they had an only son, Andrew, who was born in 1948. Twenty years later Andrew changed his surname to MacMorrough Kavanagh by deed poll.

Andrew MacMorrough Kavanagh of Borris prefers to keep a low profile and not to dwell on the nagging question of the title; Andrew sees only negative things in pushing the question of the MacMorrough Kavanagh succession at this time and does not want to become a 'pawn' of other people's strategies in the matter. He dislikes any inclination to commercialize the distinction of chief of the name. Andrew says the Irish government were wise in 1944 to re-establish the recognition of the old dynastic families and their titles – a positive action for the country's heritage and traditions and possibly a 'tourist attraction' of a special kind.

Andrew's own position – or his son Morgan's at the moment – probably cannot change unless the rule about female inheritance is reversed. He feels the Chief Herald's Office would face unwarranted turmoil if genealogical doubts and shadows were pursued at random.

Sitting in the big high-ceilinged library at Borris House, surrounded by thousands of leather-bound volumes, files, memorabilia – including his great-great-grandfather's chair-saddle perched on a mahogany stand – Andrew points to the extraordinary family documentation carrying back to the early kings of Leinster and even to their Milesian origins. There is much else to think about in the library: Does the MacMorrough Kavanagh family originate in the Ukraine? They are descended from Milesius or Míl of Spain – and strong legend says his ancestors were Scythian princes who came from the Ukraine.

BORRIS HOUSE, CO. CARLOW
Irish Architectural Archive

# CONNACHT

DESMOND RODERIC O'CONOR

# O'Conor Don

(In the case of O'Conor Don the prefix 'The' is not used; nor does the present holder of the title use the further courtesy title of Prince of Connacht used by his father, believing O'Conor Don to be, in his own words, 'historically grand enough by itself'.)

The O'Conors (Ó Conchobhair) descend from the kings of Connacht and the high kings of Ireland. Up to the fifteenth century their descent reaches back to Milesian times, three centuries before Christ. There are solid grains of fact enshrined in the myths, sagas and legends that trace this ancient House into the mists of history – even before the sons of their Galician progenitor, King Míl Espaíne (Milesius), came from the Iberian peninsula and settled in Ireland. To quote Professor Waddell of the National University of Ireland in Galway: 'The antiquity of the royal O'Conors make the Windsors look like parvenus.'

Conchobhar (d. 971), from whom the family name of O'Conor is derived, is recorded as being eighteenth in descent from Duach Galach, the first Christian king of Connacht, who died in AD 438. The O'Conors made their major political expansion in the seventh and eighth centuries and reached the crest of their power in the early twelfth century with Turlough Mór O'Conor, whose son Roderic was the last high king of Ireland. The Normans arrived in Ireland during Roderic's reign and ended the High Kingship. The O'Conors, however, remained kings of Connacht until the end of the fourteenth century; their territories and power were steadily decreased as the Norman strength in Ireland increased. Even when the O'Conors were no longer kings and the head of the House became known as O'Conor Don, they continued to be invested with all the old traditional ceremony at the historic inaugural site in Connacht down to recent times.

By the end of the seventeenth century only a fraction of their lands was held by members of the O'Conor family in County Roscommon in Connacht. Today, Clonalis alone – near the town of Castlerea – survives; the Irish Land Commission took the other property in the 1930s.

To distinguish their branch from two kindred ones – O'Conor Ruadh (red-haired) and O'Conor Sligo – the House has been styled O'Conor Don (brown-haired) since the late fourteenth century. The present O'Conor Don is one of the three recognized claimants to the High Kingship; upon the death of the immediately preceding chief of the name in July 2000, the *Irish Times* obituary stated: 'It is generally acknowledged that the holder of the (O'Conor) title would be the foremost claimant to the Irish throne, if one were proposed.'

Since the Reformation two of the three royal families descended from the high kings – The O'Brien and The O'Neill – became allied by marriage and politics with the English ascendancy in Ireland. The House of O'Conor did not do so; even during the dark days of the Penal Laws it survived uniquely attached to its old traditions. Today it is the only Catholic princely line with the family still in possession of its original ancestral land in the west of Ireland: Clonalis.

The present Clonalis House was built in the late 1800s and replaced an earlier stronghold whose ruins are still visible from the main road leading to it. The private avenue goes through a grove of trees and curves between green fields to the big comfortable residence itself, which crouches atop a small hill. Pyers Nash – who inherited the house, but not the title, from his uncle, The Reverend Charles O'Conor Don, S.J. – lives at Clonalis House with his wife and children, overseeing the demesne and its farming operations. The O'Conor-Nashs are also the custodians of the priceless relics and manuscripts that reflect the battle waged for centuries by successive generations of O'Conors to maintain a foothold against the recurrent waves of foreign rule. Clonalis is the only private historic house in Ireland open to the public (during certain months of the year) that represents the Irish rather than the Anglo-Irish tradition and illustrates the survival of this tradition from the coming of Christianity to Ireland in the fifth century up to the present day. The history of Clonalis is, in miniature, the history of Ireland.

The current holder of the title, Desmond Roderic O'Conor, has regular contact and enduring linkage with his ancient roots in Connacht; he is keenly aware of his position as head of this extraordinary family and its enduring place in history.

A tall, fit, investment banker with spectacles, thick grey hair and a scholarly mien, O'Conor Don has a ready sense of humour and a sharp intelligence that operate on a variety of levels. His blue-green eyes and the contours of his face form a look that may be unique to some of the old aristocratic families of Ireland and Britain and is rarely seen natively elsewhere in the world. A linguist, keen sportsman and amateur historian, the chief of the name was born in England in 1938; he succeeded to the title when his father, Denis Armar O'Conor died in Dublin in 2000. Desmond was brought up by his mother mainly in England, but the family also had a house in Schull, County Cork, during most of his childhood.

His mother divorced Denis and in 1943 married James Cameron, the well known British journalist and broadcaster. In 1964 Desmond married Virginia, an anglican and the daughter of Sir Michael Williams, KCMG, a former diplomat and the first British ambassador to the Vatican. (Since the Reformation the envoys from the Court of St James were Ministers only.) They have three grown children and five grandchildren. A son, Philip Hugh, the immediate heir, has two daughters.

O'Conor Don and Madam O'Conor, whose permanent residence is in Sussex, have also lived in Brazil, Peru and Central America during his career with the Bank of London, South America; Schroder Wagg; and, for the last twenty-three years, as a senior executive of Dresdner Kleinwort Benson, a powerful British-German merchant bank. Semi-retired, Desmond O'Conor, continues his role as a top echelon counsellor to this latter firm's and others' interests in South America and in Europe. O'Conor Don speaks fluent Spanish and good Portuguese; he and his wife live a sophisticated, varied life from their base in Sussex. They go to Ireland several times a year to visit relatives and friends and for Desmond to attend the meetings of the Standing Council of Irish Chiefs – as well as to go woodcock shooting in Mayo.

Denis Armar O'Conor (1912-2000), Desmond's London-born father, although chief of the illustrious, ancient Irish name, was the embodiment of both traditions but lived most of his life in Ireland. *The Daily Telegraph*, in its expansive, two-photograph obituary on 12 July 2000, described the late O'Conor Don as 'an adventurous, unrepentant representative of the old imperialist breed'. In addition to the historical references regarding the Irish royal house and to the particulars of his colourful life, the obituary further noted the late Chief's gregarious nature:

> A big man with a booming voice and a rugged, ruddy countenance, larger than life, Denis The O'Conor Don was friendly to all comers and rejoiced in convivial gatherings. He quoted poetry, had a fair appreciation of Irish whiskey and knew history. He was a crack polo player and a spirited young man with an eye for the girls. During his varied military career he lived life to the limit and often beyond ...

Schooled in England at Downside, the elite Catholic private school, and at Sandhurst, Denis O'Conor was a boxer, horseman, British army officer in India, China and the Philippines, as well as a full-fledged participant in London's and Ireland's hectic social life before and after World War II. As an expert, he taught horsemanship and was a master and judge of hunting hounds. While being a certified descendant of the Irish high kings, Denis O'Conor's immediate background and upbringing were sometimes seen as English; all who knew him, however, saw him as the epitome of an Irish gentleman and bon-vivant.

The late O'Conor Don was raised in Ireland and in north Herefordshire in the house of his maternal grandfather, Admiral the Honourable Walter Lowry-Corry, younger son of the Earl of Belmore of Castle Coole, whose family had long connections in Ireland in counties Sligo and Fermanagh. In 1936 Denis O'Conor married Elizabeth Marris, daughter of the anglican Canon of Bombay (who was so incensed at her fiancé's Catholicism that he refused to attend the wedding). Desmond, their only son born in 1938, was a baby at the time of his parents' eventual marital breakup.

In 1942 Denis O'Conor married Rosemary O'Connell Hewitt, great-granddaughter of Daniel O'Connell, the celebrated nineteenth century 'Liberator' and produced Desmond's half-brothers, Kieran and Rory. They lived in Ireland from 1945 until his death. Denis O'Conor Don became grand prior of the Ecumenical Order of St Lazarus of Jerusalem, vice chairman of the Standing Council of Irish Chiefs and an active member of many cultural and historical societies. Denis and his wife spent the later years in County Wicklow on the east coast and then in Dun Laoghaire, a suburb of Dublin, where the Dowager Madam O'Conor still resides.

While respectful of his late father's tenure as the hereditary chief, admiring his swashbuckling approach to life and clearly affectionate in his recollections, Desmond O'Conor is pragmatic and quietly disapproving about his predecessor's cavalier approach to the preservation of assets and his stewardship of the O'Conor Don's material legacy.

Denis O'Conor, together with his father – and whilst Desmond O'Conor was still a baby – were compelled to sell even the remainder interest in the entailed ancestral estate in Roscommon, which meant that neither he nor his successor would inherit Clonalis, now in possession of his kinsman, Pyers Nash.

While attentive to his family needs and prudent financial management, Desmond O'Conor Don's reflections are focused mainly on his family's longer-term past; this British-bred Catholic, the head of one of the oldest royal houses in Europe, is very Irish with his delicate amalgam of fatalism and optimism. He is well aware that the noble distinction of O'Conor Don has amazingly endured throughout Ireland's tumultuous history and he continues to seek ways to put his own passing stamp on this proud name in Ireland's history.

If history had taken a few different turns, Desmond O'Conor Don, the lean, successful banker and realist, might have been a king today. Even as recently as the 1930s a Monarchist Party was registered in Dublin; in 1937 it proposed that Owen Phelim O'Conor Don – Desmond's great-granduncle – be officially invited to be the monarch. Although the party slipped away without a trace, some irrepressible monarchists feel that it is still not totally impossible for the past to become the future for the House of O'Conor in Ireland.

CLONALIS HOUSE, CO. ROSCOMMON
Irish Architectural Archive

RORY MACDERMOT

# The MacDermot

## PRINCE OF COOLAVIN

In the mid-1960s, long before his retirement to Naas, County Kildare, Niall Anthony The MacDermot (1935-2003) had been stationed as a junior officer in Cyprus where he served in the British Royal Air Force. He – and Madam MacDermot, the former Janet Frost – liked the island and its people and, having a touch of arthritis, he craved the benefits of its Mediterranean warmth so much that they abandoned the rigours of Irish winters and moved in November 2000 to a villa in Pegeia near Paphos, not far from Nicosia, the capital. It was a dream come true for the descendant of the kings of Moylurg, Prince of Coolavin and head of his clan.

Tragically The MacDermot developed lung cancer and, after only two happy years in Cyprus, died following a brief illness.

As chief of the name, Niall had delegated much of The MacDermot's dynastic responsibilities to his son Rory (b. 1960), an enthusiastic, active tanist and to his daughter Siobhán, both of whom live in Ireland and manage all the matters relating to the MacDermot Clan Association, an international organization with many members.

No matter how settled the late head of the noble MacDermots may have felt in their new home in Cyprus, they were drawn back regularly and predictably to their ancient royal territories in the north-western part of Ireland. The MacDermot dynasty owned, ruled and clung to their birthright for seven centuries – against steadily increasing odds that ultimately prevailed. The MacDermots (who were Mulrooney before 1124) have a long history and long memories: they always go back to Coolavin.

The MacDermots and the O'Conors shared a common origin in Tadgh, King of Connacht (d. 956), who had two sons – Conchobhar (Conor) and Maolruanaidgh Mór (Mulrooney Mór). Conor succeeded his father as ruler of Connacht; his brother, Mulrooney Mór, gave up any claim to the throne of Connacht in exchange for the sovereignty of Moylurg, a sub-kingdom (under the authority of Connacht) that included a considerable portion of counties Roscommon and Sligo – still referred to as 'MacDermot's Country' – and some districts in Mayo. The MacDermots descend directly from the Moylurg dynasty of Mulrooney.

The MacDermots remained in possession of their territories up to the middle of the sixteenth century. The original family seat in Roscommon on Castle Island in Lough Key – called MacDermot's Rock even today – was held by the MacDermot Moylurg kings for over five hundred years. They were eventually overwhelmed militarily by the English and deprived of the greater part of their patrimony by the confiscations that followed the Cromwellian (1652-59) and Williamite (1689-92) wars. The last king of Moylurg, Rory MacDermot, died in 1568.

The territory seized from the princely MacDermots by Oliver Cromwell's parliamentary forces was distributed to his officers and soldiers, as well as to the English settlers who were already there. (Even before Cromwell, much of the good land around Boyle was granted by King James I to the 'foreign' King family who developed the beautiful estate of Rockingham – now the forest part of Lough Key where MacDermot Castle once stood so invulnerably.) Stripped of their ancestral lands, the king of Moylurg migrated with his family and people to a boggy area along the shores of Lough Gara in the barony of Coolavin, less than twenty miles from Boyle, nub of his former kingdom.

There was a happy but brief reversal of fortune during the Jacobite period: since The MacDermot and his nobles fought for the cause of the Catholic royal Stuarts against the Protestant William of Orange, the grateful King James II restored to them much of the territory previously confiscated by Cromwell. (The document, dated 1690, under which restoration of 'his ancient inheritances' was granted, is in the possession of Rory, the incumbent MacDermot, Prince of Coolavin.) Upon the defeat of the Stuarts and the accession to the English throne by King William IV, the MacDermots – along with many other loyal Irish Jacobites – were once again dispossessed. After James II's defeat, the Irish overall were reduced to having only one-seventh of the land they had owned. The MacDermots, with few exceptions, made no settlement with the victors regarding their faith.

'We never got any of it back,' Rory's grandfather told *The Irish Times* in an interview in 1979. The late Sir Dermot Francis The MacDermot (1906-96) had been the British Ambassador to Romania, Indonesia and Thailand before retiring to Ireland. As the bearer of both an ancient Gaelic title and a new British title, he had an ironic view of the royal MacDermots' forced transition from Moylurg to Coolavin, reported from the interview:

> The land at Coolavin – which had become our exile – was not even ours when we moved there, because, under the new English laws at that time, Catholics could not own land. So we rented it from Protestants called Ormsby. It was only four hundred acres. When I was young the family tradition was that our ancestors had become penniless princes who sat by the shores of Lough Gara reading the Latin classics. There is some truth in this. But about two centuries later, thanks to my grandfather, our family bought back that land – and more. Hugh Hyacinth O'Rorke The MacDermot, was a very prominent barrister in Dublin – and Attorney General for Ireland in the late 1800s. He also made a lot of money and it was he who built the house in Sligo which is our seat today.

Coolavin House, a handsome cut-stone residence with a Victorian formality to it, sits atop a small hill near the village of Monasteraden, County Sligo, overlooking Lough Gara in the townland of Clogher. It is close to the ruins of the previous house referred to as Old Coolavin. Beyond an iron gate a narrow unpaved driveway leads through an alley of sycamore trees and rolling parkland. Felicity, Madam MacDermot, widow of Charles, The MacDermot, Rory's late great-uncle, lives at Coolavin House and farms the land; she and her husband, a former rubber planter in Malaysia and prisoner of the Japanese in World War II, were childless. Upon Charles death in 1979, the titles – princely and chiefly – passed to his diplomat brother, Sir Dermot. The Dowager Madam Felicity MacDermot is visited often at Coolavin by other members of the family.

The MacDermot is the Prince of Coolavin. The Gaelic chieftains were forced to renounce their titles in 1585 – many in return for knighthood and baronetcy. When The MacDermot refused to do so and was compelled, with his family, to leave their estates in Moylurg and find a new, reduced location in Coolavin, it did not mean that they were divested of their royal antecedents. They continued to regard themselves as princes – as did the majority of the local people. The justification for the title of Prince of Coolavin was that, even having lost Moylurg, the MacDermots were still princes and were regarded as such by their Irish neighbours in the district of Coolavin. This sentiment persists locally today as a survival of the respect held in ancient times for persons who were, by heredity, of royal blood.

In 1944, when the Genealogical Office in Dublin gave courtesy recognition to the ancient Gaelic title of The MacDermot, it also included the recognition of the title of 'Prince of Coolavin'.

Rory's grandfather, the late Ambassador Sir Dermot MacDermot, expressed a whimsically insightful view of titles in his further comments in 1979 to Renagh Holohan, Dublin author and journalist with *The Irish Times:*

> I was knighted by Her Majesty's Government in 1962. It is just a personal reward which is nice to have. In England it empowers social status, but in Ireland 'The MacDermot' is a much older designation. Yes, we have a certain pride in our own history being so well documented that we can see who our ancestors were. Apart, though, from a certain amount of family pride, being The MacDermot now has no advantages territorially or financially – but it does keep one in touch with quite a lot of people.

From their centuries as provincial princes and regional nobles, to the modern era, the MacDermots have consistently produced worthy inheritors of their patrician tradition, strong contributors to Ireland's well-being and to the family's own substance: soldiers – from ancient Gaelic warriors to Jacobites to British military officers in World Wars I and II; parliamentarians – from the Protestant ascendancy to twentieth century independence; doctors, playwrights, senators, diplomats, lawyers, bankers and businessmen.

With his angular face – often under a brown tweed hat – his steady eyes and kindly manner, the late Niall Anthony The MacDermot of Moylurg, Prince of Coolavin, had the persona of a university don or a bishop. His quick reactions and decisive style, however, reflected his career as an RAF officer and as the entrepreneurial chief executive of his own computer software firm, Coolavin Systems Ltd in Naas where he and his wife, Jan, lived until they moved to Cyprus in 2000.

As a young boy, Niall had shared his parents' relatively peripatetic life as a diplomatic family. He was born in 1935 in the British Consulate in Yokohama and was mostly away at school or in the RAF during the latter days of his father's overseas postings. Wherever they were, Niall often said, their thoughts were never far from Coolavin, the MacDermot seat – and, so long ago, their place of exile. He had served as an active member of the Standing Council of Irish Chiefs since its inception.

Niall's son and tanist, Rory, a sturdy, brown-haired, affable man with a musketeer's moustache – and namesake of the last king of Moylurg who died 450 years ago – succeeded to the titles as well as to the custodianship of Coolavin House in February 2002. He and his young family live mostly in Killiney on Dublin Bay. His son Francis is his tanist.

The incumbent chief of the name runs a company that imports building supplies from Italy. Rory and his wife Ester, the daughter of an Italian diplomat once posted in Ireland, met as students at Trinity College Dublin. She is a senior member of the ambassador's staff at the Italian embassy (chancellery) on Northumberland Road in Dublin.

The MacDermot and his sister, Siobhán, organize the MacDermot Association Gathering every three years, which brings to Coolavin hundreds of clan members from Ireland, England, Scotland, the USA, Canada, Australia and Spain. The most recent gathering in 1999 was scheduled to coincide with the 400th anniversary of the Battle of Curlews – the last time the MacDermots and their allies defeated the English in a bloody battle in the Curlew Mountains north of Boyle. Music, recitations, set dancing, religious services, accommodations, logistics are all under Rory and Siobhán's control. In between the gatherings there is constant activity on the MacDermot website – as well as a steady stream of kin, kith, historians and the curious to Coolavin House to visit the seat of this ancient Gaelic family.

COOLAVIN HOUSE, CO. SLIGO
Irish Architectural Archive

WALTER LIONEL O'KELLY

# The O'Kelly

## OF GALLAGH AND TYCOOLY

Old film buffs, upon meeting Count The O'Kelly of Gallagh and Tycooly, would perceive in him a nostalgic blend of Wilfred Hyde-Whyte, Clive Brook and Edmund Gwenn. Of medium-build and erect in stature, with very blue eyes, Walter Lionel O'Kelly (called 'Bob' after a pony he loved as a child) has a nicely groomed white moustache to match his hair and eyebrows and an appealing way of listening closely and giving short, candid responses. He sports a vintage double-breasted navy blue blazer with well-creased grey flannel trousers and an ever-present (according to Countess or Madam O'Kelly) Trinity Association tie. Highly polished shoes reflect The O'Kelly's military service as well as his subsequent career as a business executive.

The O'Kellys have been involved in military affairs and in 'management' from earliest times. *Burke's Irish Family Records* traces their aristocratic tradition back to the sixth century:

> The pedigrees of the O'Kelly of Hy-Maine and of its chiefly family, the O'Kellys of Gallagh and Tycooly, are recorded in the Genealogical Office in Dublin. The family is alleged to have descended from Maine Óg (AD 457), first prince and founder of the illustrious house of Hy-Maine, through Ceallagh (AD 874), common ancestor of the extended O'Kelly family.

Of the several branches of the clan, the senior surviving one is O'Kelly of Hy-Maine (Úi Máine), a territory covering approximately two hundred square miles in the southern part of Roscommon and east Galway. Gallagh and Tycooly are regions of Hy-Maine that were historically identified with a specific and senior part of the family. The Hy-Maine O'Kellys have moved through the centuries with an impressive record of survival. Political agility, highlighted by strategic marriages, was a continuously important element in the noble family's strength even in pre-Norman times.

Taking their name from ancestor Ceallagh (Kelly), the twelfth Prince of Hy-Maine, the O'Kellys became petty regional sovereigns owing hereditary fealty to the territorial kings of Connacht. Like many fellow aristocrats, their marital alliances, over successive generations, serve to illustrate some of the O'Kellys' tactical prowess in protecting the future of the family: from the 1200s to 1600s the O'Kellys of Hy-Maine married into the royal families of O'Conor four times, O'Briens twice, O'Neills twice and MacDermots once. During that period they also began to establish strong links to the spreading Anglo-Norman presence in Ireland by taking as spouses members of the noble de Burgo or Bourke/Burke family (the Earls of Clanricard) five times.

The O'Kellys' history followed a pattern common to that of the other Gaelic dynastic families – initially suppressing the early alien forays into Irish territory, savagely attacking the more formidably organized Anglo-Norman forces, later opposing the invaders' settlements and finally developing with the occupiers a *modus vivendi* that ranged from mercurial violence to a fragile peace. In the seventeenth and eighteenth centuries there were significant periods when a policy of accommodation was politically profitable for both the old Gaelic aristocrats and their erstwhile (and latent) blood enemies.

As Irish history coursed its way from the intermittently turbulent pre-Norman era with many separate but interlocked monarchies and principalities, through centuries of domination, insurrection and change – and ultimately into the twentieth century with newly gained national independence for the ancient Gaelic land – the fortunes of the O'Kellys of Hy-Maine were not unlike many of the powerful native families whose entrenched hereditary power was uprooted and gradually replaced with other instruments of government and social order.

The noble legacy of the O'Kellys, princes of Hy-Maine, began to change its shape in the latter part of the sixteenth century; the crucial shift in fortune occurred when their Chief, Conor O'Kelly – finally exhausted by the force of the Tudor politico-military persuasion – submitted to Queen Elizabeth I in 1585. Under the terms of surrender-and-regrant, the O'Kellys lost their Gaelic title and the suzerainty of Hy-Maine. But after complicated protocols, the senior branch of the family was conceded a castle in Gallagh, a small townland within their old domain, plus a smaller barony in eastern Galway.

A century later these former Galwegian princes saw an opportunity to oust the Protestant Anglo-Irish dominance and to regain their confiscated property in Hy-Maine along with their proscribed noble status, by becoming officers in the Ireland-based army of the Catholic King James II. Their defeat forced William The O'Kelly to abandon Castle Gallagh and to re-establish the seat of the senior line of the ancient family in Tycooly, a quiet refuge not far from the village of Athenry.

For fifteen hundred years the O'Kellys of Hy-Maine have been historically identified with the western province of Connacht and most specifically with the modern counties of Galway and Roscommon. The last seat of The O'Kelly of Gallagh and Tycooly, was another Gallagh, near Tuam in County Galway, built by Conor or Cornelius, the present O'Kelly's great-grandfather in 1840 and destroyed by fire a century later. Galey, the previous seat, was a Norman-type defensive castle abandoned and finally destroyed three generations ago. There remains a portion of one corner still standing with a pile of stones around it. Count Robert O'Kelly, the incumbent Chief's youngest child and tanist, retrieved a large stone from the ruins of Galey, which the Chief holds as a keepsake in his residence in County Dublin.

The O'Kellys also had enduring influence both regionally and nationally, as well as in several other European countries. Throughout the struggle for survival on their native turf the family remained steadfast in their adherence to Roman Catholicism; many were (and are) members of the Sovereign Military Order of Malta. Scores of O'Kelly's were killed during the Williamite war and others fled to exile in Austria, Germany, Holland, France and Spain.

In the mid-eighteenth century, The O'Kelly, who had served as a commander in the army of Joseph III, the Holy Roman Emperor and as a Minister and Chamberlain, was ennobled by the Austrian court; John James O'Kelly of Montouban was made a count by Louis XV of France where his descendants still live; Emmanuel Francis Herbert O'Kelly was created Count O'Kelly de Galway by the King of Belgium where his descendants also still live; Dionisio O'Kelly was made a knight by the King of Spain, but his branch seems to be extinct.

Other members of the ancient Gaelic family married into Romanian (Filipescu) and Polish (Wolkonsky) nobility and remain prominent today in the cosmopolitan society of Vienna, Budapest, Paris and London. In more recent times, James John O'Kelly (d. 1916), a member of the Irish parliament, was an officer in Prince Maximilian of Hapsburg's doomed campaign to become Emperor of Mexico in the early 1800s.

His cousin, Count (of Austria) Gerald Edward O'Kelly de Gallagh (1890-1960), was Ireland's ambassador to Belgium and France.

The O'Kellys of Hy-Maine were strivers – as hereditary rulers and later as soldiers, parliamentarians, diplomats, nationalists, journalists, businessmen and religious. All O'Kellys take pride-of-clan in Sean T. O'Kelly (1883-1966), the first president of the Republic of Ireland.

Walter (Bob) Lionel O'Kelly, the current chief of the name, was born in Westmeath in 1921, educated at the elite boarding school Stonyhurst and took a civil engineering degree at Trinity College Dublin in 1943. Count The O'Kelly and Countess O'Kelly, the former June Mary Eleanor Kerans of Galway, live in Dalkey, a lovely village on the Irish Sea about eight miles south-east of Dublin. They have four children: Countess Barbara Mary Denise, Countess Eithne Mary Patricia, Countess Michele Mary Eleanor – the latter two are both nurses; and Count Robert Walter Joseph Charles, the tanist, who has three children, Francis, Maria and Colleen.

The O'Kelly does not emphasize the titles in his family, nor does he belittle them. His Gaelic title goes back a very long way. The Austrian one is newer – given to his great-great-great-grandfather, Festus, in the eighteenth century. He is the 8th count or *reichsgraf*. The titles are seldom used publicly – only on fully formal occasions.

(The O'Kelly of Gallagh and Tycooly was officially granted the courtesy of recognition as a Gaelic Chief by the Government of Ireland in 1944. The Imperial Letters Patent, issued by the Emperor of Austria in 1767, permit The O'Kelly's descendants of both genders in the male line to use the style of count or countess – the females until they marry.)

The O'Kelly served as an officer in the Royal Engineers during World War II in India and Malaya. Shortly afterwards, applying his civil and mechanical engineering skills, 'Bob' O'Kelly joined the government's energy corporation, Bord na Móna, founded in 1946 for the development of peat resources in Ireland, where he became a senior executive before retiring in 1986 after thirty-seven years of service.

The and Madam O'Kelly convey an impression of confidence, of a quiet philosophical approach to life. June, a sparkling personality, talkative and open, affectionately embellishes her husband's more laconic comments. They both have a good sense of humour, tempered by a distinct strain of Celtic fatalism.

The O'Kelly, although Roman Catholic, differs from many of his fellow claimants in his view of the imposition of primogeniture. This descendant of Prince Ceallagh of Hy-Maine believes that while Brehon tanistry may be the fairest, most ancient system in Ireland, the old Gaelic families who espouse it are swimming against the tide of reality.

Whether by primogeniture or tanistry, The O'Kelly's succession to his aristocratic legacy is unchallenged: he inherited it under both systems.

GALLAGH CASTLE, CO. GALWAY
Irish Architectural Archive

GEOFFREY PHILIP O'RORKE

# The O'Rorke

## PRINCE OF BREIFNE

While all of the hereditary chiefly families of Ireland have had tumultuous, complex relationships with their Anglo-Norman adversaries, few of the histories of these Irish aristocrats are more dramatic and varied than that of the Ó Ruaircs. Ranging from almost constant warfare to close political and marital alliances, the saga of the Ó Ruairc (O'Rourke, O'Rorke, Ruark) clan continued through alternating eras of sovereignty and wealth, exile and penury, peace and restitution. On balance, the noble Ó Ruaircs were, throughout their history, deeply anti-English and dedicated to the retention of the Gaelic monarchical system that they had been so much a part of for a millennium.

There is a certain irony in the fact that the current chief of the name, Geoffrey Philip Colomb O'Rorke, Prince of Breifne, is an 'English gentleman'. The O'Rorke was born in 1943, privately educated, and now lives in London where several of his princely Ó Ruairc predecessors died, either on the scaffold or as prisoners in the Tower, or were dispatched under mysterious circumstances. Called Philip by his family and friends, he is a senior executive with Charles Stanley and Company, an international stockbroker and asset manager on Luke Street in the City.

Philip O'Rorke, a tall, sturdy man with an air of hesitant sophistication, has a very good tailor and an excellent shirt-maker. He also has the presence of an actor: under his straight greying hair the planes of his angular face shift with the tone of the conversation; there is a vague echo of Sir John Gielgud in the deep timbre of his voice and his manner of speaking. Over lunch in 2001, The O'Rorke reflected on his family and their ancient enemy:

> During the chronic strife between us and them [the Anglo-Normans] – and many times between ourselves – over politics, land and religion – it was

not all sword play, blood and gore. Sometimes there was romance. On at least two occasions there were love affairs that had lasting repercussions. One of them affects me and my immediate family even today. And another earlier amorous family episode actually affected the course of Irish history itself …

In the late eighteenth century the chief of the name was Tadhg (Teige) Ó Ruairc, a Catholic priest in a parish near Dromahair, the ancient family seat on the Sligo/Leitrim border. Father Ó Ruairc had lodgings with the widow Gallagher and her three children. Elinor O'Rorke Gallagher, was the priest's first cousin who had joined her late husband John's faith as an anglican. Father Tadhg and Elinor, in a bloom of romance, married – following his conversion to Protestantism. He anglicized his name to the Reverend Thaddeus O'Rorke and became the curate in the Protestant church at Cong, in County Mayo. Elinor and Thaddeus had two sons of their own, both of whom became clergymen in the Church of Ireland – and one of whom is Philip O'Rorke's direct ancestor.

'Our branch of the family', said Philip, 'has been Protestant ever since the celibate Father Tadhg administered the six-pronged shock to The Ó Ruairc's family by marrying a close cousin, quitting the faith and not only joining the enemy's church but becoming a minister in it, changing his traditional name – and having children.'

The other affair of the heart cited by Philip O'Rorke happened five centuries before Father Tadhg Ó Ruairc lodged with the widow Gallagher.

In the twelfth century Tigernan (Tiernan) Ó Ruairc, king of Breifne, lived at Dromahair Castle, a long-established Ó Ruairc stronghold, with his beautiful wife Dervorgilla, daughter of the king of Meath and their numerous children. Fellow monarch and sometime ally, Dermot MacMurrough, king of Leinster, aged sixty-one, stopped at Dromahair Castle in 1162 – while, according to some annals, King Tigernan was on a pilgrimage to St Patrick's Purgatory at Lough Derg in Donegal. Dervorgilla, forty-four, eloped to Leinster with King Dermot, thereby triggering a fateful event.

In a towering rage and seeking to avenge the elopement as well as to retrieve his wife, King Tigernan of Breifne, with the support of his kinsman, Turlough O'Conor, the high king, mounted an invasion of Leinster to punish his wife's lover. King Dermot Mac Murrough, fearing the loss of his kingdom, appealed to Henry II of England to provide mercenaries to help him against the armed strength of the powerful O'Conor and Ó Ruairc dynasties.

The English king – presumably prompted by strategic reasons of his own – obliged the royal cuckold by sending to Ireland the canny, ambitious

Richard FitzGilbert de Clare, the Norman Earl of Pembroke at the head of a well trained military force. The die was cast.

Dervorgilla was dutifully returned to Castle Dromahair and her husband; she spent the last part of her life quietly with the nuns at Mellifont Abbey. The wayward queen of Breifne, in a surge of romance, had caused the Anglo-Norman invasion that irreversibly changed the course of Irish (and English) history.

In a blend of irony and historical symmetry, Dervorgilla's betrayed but avenged spouse, King Tigernan Ó Ruairc – Philip O'Rorke's direct ancestor – was slain in battle in 1172 by one of Strongbow's Norman commanders. Tigernan's nemesis, Dermot MacMurrough of Leinster would survive to play a further role in the complex saga that had just begun.

Edward MacLysaght wrote in *Irish Families* in 1957:

> In medieval times the Ó Ruaircs were one of the great princely families in Ireland. They were lords of Breifne and provided several kings of Connacht prior to the Norman invasion in the thirteenth century. At one point in history the realm of Breifne stretched from Kells in County Meath to Sligo, a territory of approximately 1400 square miles, slightly larger than Luxembourg. The Ó Ruaircs were recorded princely rulers from the 6th century and survived as hereditary chiefs and an influential aristocratic factor in Ireland for more than a thousand years.

Over the centuries, as political events in Ireland moved snail-like or cascaded one upon the other within a few generations, the Ó Ruaircs' power was shifted and metaphorized in many ways: after Oliver Cromwell's crushing mission in Ireland, like all great Gaelic families, their fortunes declined; some recouped their positions during the restoration of the Catholic Stuart dynasty and King Charles II. Scores, however, later fled to Europe. But the Ó Ruaircs, and others of that element who remained in Ireland, were once again dispossessed. The halcyon days of the once-powerful Ó Ruaircs had gone.

Many noble Ó Ruairc exiles in Europe distinguished themselves and their family as military leaders, writers and administrators. Patrick Ó Ruairc, made an imperial prince by the czar, became General-in-Chief of the Russian Empire; his descendants, until the Soviet era, were still among the important aristocratic families in Russia and Poland well into the twentieth century. Two counts Ó Ruairc served Empress Maria Teresa as Austrian ambassadors to the Court of St James in London.

Although he lives in London Philip O'Rorke is proudly conscious of his deep Irish roots and the ancient title that he bears. He commutes to his office in the financial district from South Kensington where he lives with his wife and two step-children. Madam O'Rorke, the former Penelope Barclay, sister of Peter Barclay of Towie Barclay and of that Ilk, who is the head of Clan Barclay in Scotland, is keenly interested in her own aristocratic Gaelic roots and her family's distinction in the annals of Scottish history.

The O'Rorke's tanist has not been nominated. Since he has no sons and his step-sons are not eligible, his tanist would logically be his brother's son, but it must depend ultimately, he says, on the factors of attitude and suitability – the Brehon way.

Philip O'Rorke feels, with regret, that in the future, primogeniture will finally prevail over Brehonic tanistry as the accepted system of Gaelic aristocratic succession. Like some of his fellow chiefs, he believes also that, despite, the generally excellent education system in the Republic of Ireland there is virtual ignorance of the highly civilized Gaelic era that endured for so many centuries. Philip thinks with sorrow about this gap in historical knowledge. He feels that in Ireland, aside from the universities, there seems to be little taught in schools about the eras prior to Cromwellian times: much of Gaelic history was, he said purposely stamped out by the English during the various stages of invasion and conquest

With a sad smile, The O'Rorke suggested to the author that perhaps history could simply blame Dervorgilla for all the problems between the Irish and the English.

DROMAHAIR CASTLE, CO. LEITRIM
From Francis Grose, *Antiquities of Ireland*, 1791;
Irish Architectural Archive

# Postscript

In the summer of 2003, the simmering concerns of the Chief Herald's Office regarding several of the more recent applications for courtesy recognition of the ancient Irish dynastic titles finally boiled into a decisive bureaucratic reaction: On 27 July the government of Ireland decided to end the system of officially granting recognition to the descendants of the Gaelic chiefs – a practice started in 1940 by Éamon de Valera's administration. Brendan O'Donoghue, the Chief Herald and the Council of Trustees of the National Library to whom he reported, recommended that the practice be terminated. Immediately prior to the decision John O'Donoghue (no kin), a government Minister, said in an interview with the *Sunday Times*: 'Since the practice of courtesy recognition has little in common with a modern state, (the practice) should be discontinued.'

The announcement by the government was received by the Irish public in various ways. Many were bemused, indeed amazed, that such an issue – or its components – even existed; others thought the decision was long overdue; and the more history-oriented public sentiment felt that the Office of the Chief Herald, i.e. government itself, had over-reacted.

Sean J. Murphy, MA, head and sole employee of the private Centre for Irish Genealogy and Historical Studies in Dublin, an occasional thorn in the side of the Chief Herald and a prime participant in exposing the fraudulent MacCarthy claim in 1999, told the *Sunday Times* that he regretted the government's decision to end their long involvement with validation of the Gaelic chiefs:

> The reality is that Terence MacCarthy and merely a few other spurious or questionable claimants succeeded in subverting the respected system of recognizing Chiefs. That should be cause for restoring and updating rather than abandoning the system. The floodgates could now be opened to bogus and fantasy Chiefs. The fact that a number of sham pedigrees, arms and titles

were entered in the records of the Office of the Chief Herald, should incite some kind of official inquiry into the administration of these departments (of the government).

The Irish government had its own rationale. Change was sought by the government, reported *The Irish Times*, due to legal difficulties surrounding courtesy recognition of the titles. Also, questions began to be asked about validity of some titles and the integrity of the honour system, tinged with disgrace over the MacCarthy case. The Office of the Chief Herald and the government suffered brief but stinging public embarrassment.

The MacCarthy fraud notwithstanding, the main stated reason for the Cabinet decision in 2003 was that the government believes it has no statutory power to give out the hereditary titles, so the chiefs of the name were told that state recognition no longer has any validity status.

Under the light of scholarly scrutiny the lineages of the majority of the ancient Irish chiefs are judged to be flawless. Among the twenty chiefs of the name five lines of descent have some lingering questions: in the cases of The O'Carroll, The Maguire and The O'Long, a few missing key documents are being traced; with The O'Rorke and The MacDonnell, interpretation and determination of seniority are being studied, with no implications of fraud or chicanery. Inquiries are being pursued by the families concerned.

Among a few members of the Standing Council of Irish Chiefs, there is a feeling that their organization would be better served by adopting an expanded charter, a broader definition of eligibility: a bigger tent, so to speak, which would include not only Gaelic ruling families, but the senior surviving representatives of the later Norman-dominated Irish dynasties: for example, the FitzGeralds (Desmond FitzGerald, Knight of Glin; and Lord FitzGerald, Knight of Kerry, the 'White Knight'), the Joyces (whose Chief, is by, courtesy, already a member of the Council) and perhaps some dormant titles.

Countering this ecumenical attitude, there is a strong ethno-centric conviction among most of the members of the Standing Council of Irish Chiefs that the first prerequisite for inclusion is a predominant and direct Gaelic lineage. Otherwise, these genealogical purists say, the historical point is lost – along with an understanding of the Irish nation's elder bloodlines.

The Standing Council has pondered over the implications of the government's decision and its effect on the future of the chiefly families' traditional position in Ireland's long history. It is probable that the government's ruling regarding official recognition would make no difference to the families' status; general recognition or appreciation of their positions could be reinforced by other means – including the council's own Committee on Privilege, which would take on the responsibility of vetting applications made by those wishing to prove their claim to a chieftaincy.

Arthur Beesley, political reporter of *The Irish Times*, wrote on 28 July 2003, that 'official courtesy recognition provides no benefits or perks of any kind'. So one could ask how a political body can – or would want to – legislate arbitrarily matters relating to its own country's history?

In the French Republic royal and noble lineages and titles are not officially recognized – by parliamentary courtesy or otherwise; they are, however, widely accepted and usually respected by the public as part of the historic national fabric, and are capitalized upon by historical associations, academe, tourist boards, agencies and businesses. A number of *bona-fide* social organizations and publishing houses are also chartered to foster and protect the integrity of French dynastic lineages: Association d'Entraide de la Noblesse Francaise, Institut de la Maison de Bourbon, Institut Napoleon, Le Nobiliaire, L'Almanac de Gotha, Le Bottin Mondain and further such dedicated enterprises. Similar associations operate profitably and proudly in Italy, Portugal, Austria and other former monarchies without prejudice or opposition.

As in other parts of Europe, dynastic hereditary rulerships in Ireland lasted far longer than any other form of government. Over sixty years ago the new Irish state had the confidence and perspective to salute officially its ancient native monarchical past by acknowledging the surviving senior direct descendants of the Irish royal houses. (History, of course, is awash with charlatans and poseurs who were seduced by the magnetism of high office and royal lineage. These impostors were, however, mostly minor footnotes, rarely notable figures.) Ireland's own history is much too complex and splendid to be 'readjusted' for reasons of current bureaucratic pique. In January 2004 Desmond FitzGerald, Knight of Glin, expressed his views on the matter: 'It is historically improper that these ancient and romantic titles are no longer officially recognized by the [Irish] State – obviously and only because of the abuse by certain individuals in the recent past.'

Observers say that, by ceasing the official courtesy recognition of the Gaelic chiefs, the Irish government, through the Office of the Chief Herald, may now be faced with a clutch of spurious applications for grant of arms. Some of the already recognized chiefs, who have had doubts cast on their authenticity, may wish to take legal action with the government to clarify their positions – expensive distractions that no administration would welcome.*

The ancient ruling dynasties are an integral part of Ireland's past. There is a general feeling, among a number of historians and others who follow such matters, that the certifiable senior descendants should be officially acknowledged in some fashion, rather than marginalized and should be recognized for what they are – the living remnants of the vanished Gaelic kingdoms.

* Brendan O'Donoghue, former Chief Herald, has said anyone, male or female, can apply for a grant of arms; a grant of arms does not confer or imply any particular status or rank.

# Bibliography and Further Reading


Bassy, Frederick, *Irish Conspiracies* (London 1910).
Beckett, J.C., *A Short History of Ireland* (London 1958).
—— *The Anglo-Irish Tradition* (London 1976).
Bence-Jones, Mark, *Twilight of the Ascendancy* (London 1987).
Berresford Ellis, Peter, *Erin's Blood Royal* (London 1999).
—— *Eyewitness to Irish History* (London 2004).
Blake Foster, Charles French, *Irish Chieftains* (Dublin 1872).
Breffney, Brian de, *Castles of Ireland* (London 1977).
*Burke's Irish Family Records* (London 1976).
*Burke's Landed Gentry of Ireland* (London 1958).
*Burke's Peerage* (London 1970).
Cruise-O'Brien, Conor and Maire, *The Story of Ireland* (New York 1972).
Curley, Walter J.P., *Monarchs-in-Waiting* (New York 1973).
Curtayne, Alice, *The Irish Story* (New York 1960).
Duffy, Patrick J., Edwards, David and Fitzpatrick, Elizabeth, *Gaelic Ireland (1250-1650): Land, Lordship and Settlement* (Dublin 1999).
Fallon, Niall, *The Armada in Ireland* (London 1978).
Fenyvesi, Charles, *Royalty in Exile* (London 1981).
Freeman, A. Martin (ed.), *The Annals of Connacht* (Dublin 1941).
Gadd, Ronald P., *The Peerage of Ireland* (Dublin 1988).
Gray, Tony, *No Surrender: The Siege of Londonderry, 1689* (London 1975).
Hayes, Richard, *The Last Invasion of Ireland* (Dublin 1937).
Hennessey, Maurice, *The Wild Geese: The Irish Soldier in Exile* (London 1973).
Hickey, Des and Smith, Gus, *Flight from the Celtic Twilight* (New York 1973).
Holohan, Renagh and Williams, Jeremy, *The Irish Chateaux* (Dublin 1989).
McCullough, David W., *Wars of the Irish Kings* (New York 2000).
MacDermot, Dermot, *MacDermot of Moylurg* (Leitrim 1996).
MacLysaght, Edward, *Irish Families* (Dublin 1957).
MacManus, Seamus, *The Story of the Irish Race* (New York 1966).
Mason, Thomas, *The Islands of Ireland: Their Scenery, People, Life and Antiquities* (London 1936).
Moody, T.W., *The Ulster Question* (Dublin 1974).

—— and Martin, F.X., *The Course of Irish History* (Dublin 1967).
Mullen, Michael, *The Flight of the Earls* (Dublin 1998).
Murtaugh, Paul, *Your Irish Coats-of-Arms* (New York 1959).
Nicholls, Kenneth, *Gaelic and Gaelicized Ireland in the Middle Ages* (Dublin 2003).
O'Brien, Donough, *History of the O'Briens From Brian Bóroimhe AD 1000 to AD 1945* (London 1949).
O'Brien, Grania, *These My Friends and Forebears: The O'Briens of Dromoland* (Clare 1991).
O'Connell, Daniel, *Ireland and the Irish: a Memoir on Ireland, Native and Saxon* (Dublin 1843).
O'Hart, John, *Irish Landed Gentry: When Cromwell Came to Ireland* (Dublin 1884).
Simms, J.G., *Jacobite Ireland 1685-91* (London 1969).
Somerset Fry, Peter and Fiona, *A History of Ireland* (New York 1988).
Vere White, Terence de, *Ireland* (London 1968).
Watson, Mark, *Royal Families Worldwide* (London 1999).
Weir, Hugh W. L. (ed.), *Ireland: A Thousand Kings* (Clare 1988).

## FURTHER READING

(Standard sources of historical information regarding the royal Irish dynasties and their descendants are included in the preceeding Bibliography. The following additional publications and family papers has been provided principally but not exclusively by some of the incumbent chiefs of the name.)

### FOX

Cooke, Thomas Lawlor, *History of Birr* (Dublin 1875).
Crisp, Frederick Arthur, and Howard, Joseph J., *Visitation of Ireland,* vol. 6 (London 1918).
Stone, M. E., *Some Notes on the Fox Family of Kilcoursey in King's Co.* (Chicago 1890).

### MACDERMOT

*Annals of Loch Cé: A Chronicle of Irish Affairs from AD 1014 to AD 590* (London 1871).
Crisp, Frederick Arthur, and Howard, Joseph J., *Visitation of Ireland,* vol. 6 (London 1918).

### MACDONNELL

Fitzgerald, Walter, *The MacDonnells of Tinnakill Castle* (Kildare 1915).
Hill, George, *Notice of the Clan Iar Vór, Clan-Donnell Scots, Especially of the Branch Settled in Ireland* (Belfast 1861).
—— *An Historical Account of the MacDonnells of Antrim* (Belfast 1873).
—— *Chief of the Antrim MacDonnells Prior to Sorley Boy* (Belfast 1859).
—— *Clan Donnell Scots: Irish Branch* (Belfast 1861).
McDonnell, Hector, *The Wild Geese of the Antrim MacDonnells* (Dublin 1996).

MCGILLYCUDDY OF THE REEKS

Bence-Jones, Mark, *A Guide to Irish Country Houses* (London 1990).

Brady, William, *The McGillycuddy Papers* (London 1932).

MACMORROUGH KAVANAGH

Furlong, Nicholas, *Dermot, King of Leinster and the Foreigners* (Dublin 1973).

—— *A Foster Son for a King* (Tralee 1986).

*The Irish Genealogist,* vol. 5, no. 5 (1979).

*The Irish Genealogist,* vol. 5, no. 6 (1979).

*The Irish Genealogist,* vol. 6, no. 2 (1981).

McCormick, Donald, *The Incredible Mr Kavanagh* (London 1960).

Moore, Donal, *English Action, Irish Reaction: The MacMorrough Kavanaghs 1530–1630* (Maynooth 1987).

MAGUIRE

Livingstone, Peader, *The Fermanagh Story* (Donegal 1969).

Maguire, The, 'The historic Maguire chalices', due 2004.

Maguire, Thomas, *Fermanagh: Its Native Chiefs and Clans* (Omagh 1954).

O'Laughlin, Michael, *County Fermanagh and Louth Genealogy and Family History Notes* (Dublin 2002).

O'BRIEN

Lindsay, W.A., *The O'Briens* (London 1876).

O'Donoghue, John, *Historical Memoir of the O'Briens* (Dublin 1860).

Rutherfurd, Edward, *The Princes of Ireland* (New York 2004).

Walsh, Paul, *Irish Chiefs and Leaders* (Dublin 1960).

O'CALLAGHAN

Crisp, Frederick Arthur, and Howard, Joseph J., *Visitation of Ireland,* vol. 1 (London 1898).

Webb, Herbert G., *The Chieftains of Pobul-I-Callaghan, Co. Cork* (Cork 1897).

O'CARROLL

Carroll, Charles, *Life Correspondence of Charles Carroll* (New York 1898).

Geiger, Mary Virginia, *Daniel Carroll II: One Man and His Descendants 1730-1798* (Baltimore 1979).

Gleeson, John, *History of Ely O'Carroll Territory of Ancient Ormond* (Dublin 1915).

Hoffman, Ronald, *Princes of Ireland, Planters of Maryland: A Carroll Saga, 1500-1782* (London 2000).

O'Carroll, 'The Milesians of Ireland' (Family papers 1994).

O'Carroll, E., 'Pedigree of the O'Carroll family' (Family papers 1883).

O'Hart, John, *Irish Pedigrees* (Dublin 1888).

'Eile: Kings and chiefs of Eile O'Carroll' (Family papers 1983).

'Septs of the Midlands and English of the Pale' (Family papers 1908).

O'CONNOR (O'CONOR)

Crisp, Frederick Arthur, and Howard, Joseph J., *Visitation of Ireland*, vol. 6 (London 1918).

Foster, R.F., *The Oxford History of Ireland* (Oxford 2001).

O'Conor Don, Charles, *The O'Conors of Connacht* (Dublin 1892).

O'Conor, Roderic, *Lineal Descent of the O'Connors of Co. Roscommon* (Dublin 1861).

O'DOGHERTY

Bonner, Brian, *The Homeland of Ó Dochartaigh* (Limerick 1985).

d'Angerville, Count (ed.), *The Royalty, Peerage and Nobility of Europe* (Monaco 1997).

Day, Angelique, and Williams, Patrick, *Ordnance Survey: Memoirs of Ireland, 1830,* vol. 31 (Belfast 1990).

FitzGerald, J., *Inis Owen: Land of The O'Dogherty* (Foyle 1934).

Grehan, Ida, *Irish Family Names* (London 1973)

Grenham, John, *Irish Family Names* (London 1997).

Harkin, Michael, *Inishowen: Its History, Traditions and Antiquities* (Donegal 1935).

Matthews, Anthony, *Origin of The O'Dogherty* (Dublin 1978).

Ó Dochartaigh, Seoirse Fionbarra, *O'Doherty: People and Places* (Clare 1998).

O'Dogherty, Pascual, 'Pedigree of the O'Dochartaigh princes and lords of Inis Eoghain' (Family papers 2004).

Sainero, Ramón, *Leabhar Ghabhala, El Libro de las Invasiones* (Spain 1988).

Sainero, Ramón, *La Huella Celtica en España e Irlanda* (Spain 1987).

O'DONNELL

Reilly, Robert, *Red Hugh: Prince of Donegal* (North Dakota 1997).

Simms, Katharine, *From Kings to Warlords: The Changing Political Structure of Gaelic Ireland in the Later Middle Ages* (Dublin 2000).

Thornton-Cook, Elsie Prentys, *John O'Donnell of Baltimore: His Forbears and Descendants* (London 1934).

O'DONOGHUE

Gorges, Marg, *Killarney* (London 1912).

Hall, Mr and Mrs S. C., *A Week in Killarney* (London 1850).

Lever, Charles, *The O'Donoghue* (Dublin 1845).

O'Connor, Peader, *Irish Family Names* (Cork 1991).

O'Donoghue, Rod, *O'Donoghue People and Places* (Clare 1999).

O'DONOVAN

*Burke's Peerage and Baronetage* 1902–1907 edition, (London 1907).

Healy, James N., *Castles of County Cork* (Cork 1988).

O'Donovan, Daniel, *Sketches in Carbery* (Dublin 1878).

O'Donovan, John (ed.), *The Annals of the Kingdoms of Ireland, by the Four Masters* (Dublin 1851).

O'Murchadha, Diarmuid, *Family Names of County Cork* (Dublin 1985).

O'GRADY

Crisp, Frederick Arthur, and Howard, Joseph J., *Visitation of Ireland*, vols 4/5 (London 1911).

O'Laughlin, Michael, *The Families of County Limerick* (Dublin 1999).

O'KELLY

Crisp, Frederick Arthur, and Howard, Joseph J., *Visitations of Ireland*, vol. 4 (London 1904).

Kelly, Richard J., *The O'Kellys of Gallagh, Counts of the Holy Roman Empire* (Galway 1904).

—— *Notes on the Family of O'Kelly* (Galway 1905).

O'LONG

Collins, John T., 'The Longs of Muskerry and Kinalea', *Journal of the Cork Historical and Archeological Society,* vol. 1 (1946).

O'Long, The, 'Irish chiefship: The O'Long', *Journal of the Cork Historical and Archeological Society,* vol. 105 (2000).

Stalley, Roger (ed.), *Daniel Grose (c.1766–1838): The Antiquities of Ireland, A Supplement to Francis Grose* (Dublin 1991).

O'MORCHOE

Culliton, Edward, *Celtic and Early Christian Wexford* (Dublin 1999).

Furlong, Nicholas, *A History of County Wexford* (Dublin 2003).

Murphy, Hilary, *Families of County Wexford* (Dublin 1986).

*Chronicles of County Wexford brought down to the Year 1877*. Compiled by George Griffith and printed at the Watchmen Office, Enniscorthy –

O'Byrne, Emmett, *War, Politics and the Irish of Leinster, 1156–1606* (Dublin 2003).

O'NEILL

Cohen, Marilyn, *The Warp of Ulster's Past* (Manchester 1996).

Crawford, Robert George, *Loyal to King Billy: A Portrait of the Ulster Protestants* (London 1967).

Holland, Jack, *Hope against History: The Course of Conflict in Northern Ireland* (London 1999).

# Index